Pray Now

2012

Daily Devotions on the Theme of Time

Published on behalf of the
THE PRAY NOW GROUP

SAINT ANDREW PRESS
Edinburgh

First published in 2011 by
Saint Andrew Press
121 George Street
Edinburgh EH2 4YN

Copyright © Pray Now Group, Faith Expressions Team, Mission and Discipleship Council, The Church of Scotland, 2011

ISBN 978 0 86153 597 2

British Library Cataloguing in Publication Data
A catalogue record for this book is available from the British Library

It is the publisher's policy to only use papers that are natural and recyclable and that have been manufactured from timber grown in renewable, properly managed forests. All of the manufacturing processes of the papers are expected to conform to the environmental regulations of the country of origin.

Typeset by Waverley Typesetters, Warham
Manufactured in Great Britain by Bell & Bain Ltd, Glasgow

Contents

Preface

If this generation is going to be famed in history for its desire for immediacy, then let the church be known through this same era for its invitation to find time. It is indeed an invitation to take what is most sacred to us: time to grow in God; time to renew our relationships; time to explore our faith; and time to spend together, all of which is never done in an instant, and know the generosity of a God who has taken time, more time than the universe has yet made possible, to love us, bless us and grow with us.

Each day's phrases and images from this book offer a moment with the God of Time. That in itself makes this a rich enough resource. Add to that the words and stories and emotions each day contains for us, knowing that there is a whole body of people engaging each day in their own place, making that same time to seek and know and spend in God, turns this resource into its own unique community.

So I hope both the words and silence these pages offer, daily shape time for you, bending it a little towards God each day, offering space and love, to be still and to know the very God who holds each day and every moment.

REV. RODDY HAMILTON
Vice-Convener
Faith Expression Team 2012

Using this Book

There is a time for everything,
and a season for every activity under the heavens

~ Ecclesiastes 3:1 ~

The theme for this year is 'Time'. We all measure time in the same way, but how we experience time and its passing are dependent on our age and individual circumstances. The writers of *Pray Now* took for their inspiration the well-known verses from the Book of Ecclesiastes. Chapter 6 verses 1–8 were made even more familiar in 1959 when Pete Seeger used them in his song 'Turn, turn, turn' which became a classic when it was an international hit for The Byrds in 1965.

We have taken the couplets, beginning 'A time to be born and a time to die …' and used each part for the title of one of the 31 days of prayers offered. The centre of the book, Day 18, is entitled 'Chronos and Kairos' – the two words that the ancient Greeks used for time. *Chronos* refers to chronological or sequential time measured by fixed intervals from seconds to years to eons.

Kairos is a moment of qualitative rather than quantitative time when something special happens. In the New Testament, *kairos* means an appointed time when God acts to fulfil God's purpose. For example, the coming of Christ is a kairos moment – John the Baptist announces the kairos when he says 'The time has come … the Kingdom of God has come near' (Mark 1:15).

When we pray we often desire for God to respond or act at the time of our choosing, but perhaps it is the other way round – we respond or act as a result of prayer at the time of God's choosing! The book begins and ends with 'Alpha' and 'Omega' – as the hymn 'Of the Father's love begotten' tells us: 'He is Alpha and Omega, He the source the ending He' (*CH4* 319 verse 1).

As always, this book is an invitation: readers are invited to use the contents as a stimuli for prayerful reflection. We have welcomed all the feedback we have received and we thank those who took the time to communicate with us. In response, we have returned to a smaller sized book that fits easily into a pocket or small bag. We have also evolved the content of the book to include:

- a title from *Ecclesiastes 3:2–8* below which is the scriptural verse that has stimulated the content for the day
- a short meditation
- a short prayer
- suggestions for Scriptural reading
- prayers for others that now go beyond the people and offices of the Church of Scotland (specific prayers for Kirk staff and missionaries can be found on the Church of Scotland website under "Worship")
- a blessing.

Each day may be taken as a whole, or readers may choose to reflect only on the meditation to prompt personal prayer and next month use the suggested prayer for reflection. Many people use *Pray Now* as an individual resource, praying in a chosen place at home or work or outside or while travelling. But *Pray Now* is also a useful resource for:

- prayer pairs or a prayer group – in a home or church
- midweek or shorter acts of worship with the addition of a hymn and perhaps a discussion element
- as opening devotions at the beginning of any meeting that you might hold
- meditations may also be used in main acts of worship if they help the congregation to explore or reflect on one of the Bible readings for the day
- a summer series preaching on the theme of 'Time' could utilise some of the content of this year's *Pray Now*.

Whatever way you choose to use this book, let's be thankful to God for the gift of prayer and of time itself. As the American writer and poet Henry Van Dyke put it,

Time is too slow for those wait,
too swift for those who fear,
too long for those who grieve,
too short for those who rejoice,
but for those who love
time is eternity.

REV. CAROL FORD
Convener of the Pray Now *Group 2012*

Ecclesiastes 3:1–8

For everything there is a season, and a time for every matter under heaven:
a time to be born, and a time to die;
a time to plant, and a time to pluck up what is planted;
a time to kill, and a time to heal;
a time to break down, and a time to build up;
a time to weep, and a time to laugh;
a time to mourn, and a time to dance;
a time to throw away stones, and a time to gather stones together;
a time to embrace, and a time to refrain from embracing;
a time to seek, and a time to lose;
a time to keep, and a time to throw away;
a time to tear, and a time to mend;
a time to keep silence, and a time to speak;
a time to love, and a time to hate;
a time for war, and a time for peace.

Days of the Month

ALPHA

'I am the Alpha and the Omega,' says the Lord God, 'who is, and who was, and who is to come, the Almighty'.

~ Revelation 1:8 ~

Meditation

Before the instant
before which there is *no* instant,
You are.
Eternally begetting, begotten, proceeding: God.
And you, you-without-beginning, make a beginning. *You speak your word.*

Our utterances unfold in time: sound succeeds sound, word succeeds word:
but *time* is bracketed, framed, by your articulations; your Word:
Alpha, Omega; the first, the last …

God spoke, and all came to be.
Joyfully expanding, into and out of, yet always within, itself,
the universe unfolds.

Alpha. This beginning, which we hail as *your* beginning of all things.
Instinctively, we locate it *behind us*, receding.
It slips away from us, and with it, you,
God on an ever-receding horizon …

Yet *all our moments*,
not merely the first,
proceed from you.
Moment to moment, instant to instant,
everything we have, everything we are,
being – all being; our being; *my* being – is your gift,
cosmic yet intimate Alpha, Being-in-yourself.

And so you speak your Word – made flesh – into our flux of moments, our time.

Your Alpha is for us a new beginning.
And we are a new creation.

Prayer

Creator God,
are You like a toy maker –
the universe Your wind-up
clockwork toy?
Do you watch it and us
proceeding away from You
until we run down?
Or are You like a parent
arms open
encouraging a barely toddling infant
to take tottering steps towards You?
Or is the same question
what am I like?
Am I like a clockwork toy?
Or am I like a child of God?

Please God,
help me to toddle off
in the right direction. AMEN.

Suggested Scripture Readings

Revelation 1:4–8   *'Alpha and Omega'*
Psalm 87   *'The ever-contemporary origin and source'*

Prayers for Others

For those just starting their journey of faith and for those seeking a new beginning.

Blessing

God,
Then, now and always the creator of all things,
then, now and always the Word spoken and speaking in
      creation,
then, now and always the Lord and Giver of Life,
bless and keep you. AMEN.

'A TIME TO BE BORN ...'

So in the course of time Hannah conceived and gave birth
to a son. She named him Samuel, saying, 'Because I asked
the LORD for him'.

~ 1 Samuel 1:20 ~

Meditation

For days, weeks, months
you are mine alone.
Held within my inner core
I whisper to you,
sing to you,
tell you stories of how you came to be.
You feed upon the goodness I consume,
and as you leap
within,
I guess you sense
the excitement of your arrival
in the voices beyond your abode.

Birthed on muscular waves,
crashing into light and colour,
your promise is released into the world.
For the small community around you,
you are the thrill of opportunity
to show love for creation
in your moulding and shaping.

Prayer

Divine Midwife,
mopping the sweat laid brow of creation,
You are the instigator of change
releasing new possibilities
with every birthing moment.
You inspire us to be involved
in your gift of potential;
to nurture the vulnerable and fragile;
to encourage growth and strength;
to recognise what we might learn

from the gift before us.
May you inspire us
to cherish
the uncertainty of birth. AMEN.

Suggested Scripture Readings

I Samuel 1:9–20   *'The Birth of Samuel'*
John 3:1–10   *'Jesus teaches Nicodemus'*

Prayers for Others

Remember those who give birth to children and ideas, and those who offer support during the labour.

Blessing

In the birth of each child, idea and opportunity
may God guide
the growth and life,
that will bring blessing
to creation. AMEN.

'A TIME TO DIE …'

If we live, we live to the Lord; and if we die, we die to the Lord. So, whether we live or die, we belong to the Lord.

~ Romans 14:8 ~

Meditation

You have taught me how to live
in your dying.
Your journey towards
an end that you knew was coming
was a humbling experience,
for you shared with us the news
that death was knocking
at your door.
In your honesty
of your uncertainty about the final frontier
towards which you travelled,
people took time to reflect with you
about how you had touched their lives.
There were memories of how their lives had become
intermingled with yours.
You took time to share out your possessions,
ensuring that each gift you gave
would carry memory
or be of use
as the missing of you
took hold of us.

You taught me how to live in your dying:
remembering that others matter;
that the stories we share
shape the paths of those we love;
that the gifts we give
may offer comfort and healing.

And in the moment of death
you lived the faith that you had found in life
and placed yourself in your Lord's hands.

Prayer

Lord of life and death,
with all my fears of the unknown
I place myself in your hands
and search for the assurance
that you will be with me
in the 'valley of the shadow of death'.
As you have shaped my life
with Christ's story
taking form in simple word and actions,
may you shape my death.
In the expressions
of care and love from others
may I see your face
easing fear,
caressing pain,
acknowledging the hope and expectation
of resurrection in Christ's name. AMEN.

Suggested Scripture Readings

> Romans 14:5–11   *'Living as God's people'*
> Ruth 1:11–17   *'Ruth chooses to go to Naomi'*

Prayers for Others

Remember those who are dying and those who will miss
them. For those who offer comfort to those with terminal
conditions, and those who offer spiritual guidance to those
who are dying.

Blessing

> Bless all whose will or name or love
> reflects the grace of heaven above.
> Though unacclaimed by earthly powers,
> your life through theirs has hallowed ours. AMEN.

(John L. Bell)

'A TIME TO PLANT ...'

When a farmer plows for planting, does he plow continually?
Does he keep on breaking up and harrowing the soil?

~ Isaiah 28:24 ~

Meditation

Putting our hands in the soil
using tools and fingers to grab and dig
selecting seed or bulb or cutting –
when we plant we care for the plant
and we care what happens to it,
we care how it flourishes or perishes,
how we may protect it and nurture it
how it looks or tastes,
but we must also know when to leave it alone,
when our role as one who plants must become that
of one who waits.

Often we invest time, energy and work
into tasks that will not show fruit until much later,
perhaps seasons, years or lifetimes away.
Let us celebrate, then, the planting
as well as the gathering in.
Only you see inside the earth,
inside our minds and hearts
only you will see all things to their conclusions.

Let us take comfort in this, just as we take comfort in the
    renewal of spring
let us feel joy at the sowing and hope for a harvest.

Prayer

Lord, you are more than a gardener.
You watched me in the womb, the earth of my mother,
from seed, to shoot, to person-plant,
growing and changing
needing light,
air
and water.

Each time I begin something new
remind me of the sanctity of care I received
in the womb
and in your love. AMEN.

Suggested Scripture Readings

Isaiah 28:23–9   *'To plow and to plant'*
1 Corinthians 3:1–9   *'God makes it to grow'*

Prayers for Others

For everyone who has new ideas, begins new things, blazes
new trails, even in difficult ground.

Blessing

Ideas shoot up like crocuses in our minds
hope like an acorn in our hearts
and our souls are sewn in love, love, love.
Bless the new things we begin
and the new things that we feel,
bless my work that it be true, and may the beneficiaries
be as blessed in the rewards as I was in the planting.
May every seed of your spirit
come to flower in the earth of myself. AMEN.

'A TIME TO PLUCK UP WHAT IS PLANTED ...'

My eyes will watch over them for their good, and I will bring them back to this land. I will build them up and not tear them down; I will plant them and not uproot them.

~ Jeremiah 24:6 ~

Meditation

The Lord casts his eyes across the garden
and uproots and replants
where change will bear fruit.

In the garden
I struggle,
uprooting what looks like weeds
and what has failed to grow.
Uprooting can bring rejuvenation,
for in another part of the garden –
in different soil and climate –
what was weak and failing
can burst to life.

In uprooting myself
will the future bear fruit?
I fear the lost friendships and support
that have allowed me to grow;
and wonder what a different soil and climate
may offer my newly watered roots.

Prayer

Lord of creation,
I find it hard to place the future in your hands
and offer you complete commitment
over what is best for the future.

In this place I am comfortable:
strengthened by those around me
who offer me security and protection;
drawing what I need to grow and be creative

from the resources that surround me.
To be uprooted from this place of being
frightens me.

May I be strengthened with the Lord's Spirit of courage:
to face the fears of leaving behind what I love and know;
to place my roots in new ground;
to be tended by God's love;
and find what fruits of faith might grow. AMEN.

Suggested Scripture Readings

Jeremiah 24:3 –7   *'God's care of the exiles from Judah'*
Matthew 2:13–15   *'The escape to Egypt'*

Prayers for Others

Pray for all of those who are living as refugees, or in exile;
and remember those who offer support and welcome.

Blessing

> May God's blessing be found
> in all newly planted roots;
> May Christ's love be offered
> in the care that encourages growth;
> May the Spirit's energy bear fruit
> as the buds of new life appear. AMEN.

'A TIME TO KILL …'

Then he (Saul) said to me, 'Come, stand here by me and kill me!

I'm in the throes of death, but I'm still alive'. So I stood beside him, and killed him.

~ 2 Samuel 1:9–10a ~

Meditation

You, Lord Jesus:
bringer of good news to the poor,
releaser of captives,
liberator of the oppressed –
love is Your being,
and justice is Your practice.
You offer life in all its fullness.

Is there a time to kill?

'You shall not murder' –
so crystal clear:
not even a life for a life
You taught us.

But what happens
when a poor soul struggles
with a pain-imprisoned body
or a dementia oppressed mind
and suffering goes beyond
human endurance –
is that the time
when the final act
of justice and healing
is to release someone
from terminal torment?

Is there a time to kill in mercy?

Forgive me for asking Lord.
But it's unbearable to watch
someone You love
bound in hell.

Prayer

Dear Christ, guide us, we pray
in matters of life and death.
For we act as God when we create lives,
we act as God when we save lives,
we act as God when we pluck life from the womb.
And now, faced with cries for legal euthanasia,
we need Your Spirit's help.
May we do what we believe is God's will.
And if, in love, we get it wrong
be there for us on the Cross. AMEN.

Suggested Scripture Readings

2 Samuel 1:5–10   *'The mercy killing of Saul'*
Exodus 21:12–26   *'Laws on killing and violence'*

Prayers for Others

Pray for those who professionally or personally are making
life-and-death decisions, and for the church, that we may be
the voice and body of Christ to those who are dying.

Blessing

May God bless You
to act justly
love tenderly
and walk humbly
in His name. AMEN.

'A TIME TO HEAL ...'

*A man with leprosy came and knelt before him and said,
'Lord, if you are willing, you can make me clean'. Jesus
reached out his hand and touched the man. 'I am willing,'
he said. 'Be clean!'*

~ Matthew 8:2–3 ~

Meditation

It was the right moment.
Rooted in seeds of hope
scattered and sown with hopefulness;
birthed in brave words
breathed through brokenness;
given life in truth's touch
and talk of wholeness.
    And he waited.

And at that moment
long held hurts shed their skin,
falling to the earth like dust.
And he rose again
evidence of a new relationship
not carved in stone but forged in faith;
not confined to tomes and temples
but let loose to run riot
and wreak the havoc of healing.
    And all was well.

At any moment, silent or startling
desired or denied, in slow mending
or in the soul's sudden surge,
healing seeks the aching spaces
and waits.

Prayer

We're not good at waiting, Lord,
for what we think we need.
We read of miracles and expect them in our own lives.
Are we not the leper aching to be well?

Are we not the blind man yearning to see?
Do we not clutch at your cloak
and demand to be accepted?

And in our expectation
that all must be well
we shun you, we fail to see you
we let you go and nurse our wounds
like faith trophies.

At any moment may we chase our doubts
choose our words and chance our healing.
It is ours for the asking
ours for the taking
yours for the giving.

But in your own time, Lord,
for only you know the right time. AMEN.

Suggested Scriptural Readings

Matthew 8:1–4   *'Jesus heals a leper'*
Isaiah 58:8–9   *'A promise of help and healing'*

Prayers for Others

Pray for those who seek healing, be it physical, mental or spiritual; and pray for a blessing on the hands that offer it.

Blessing

Thou, my soul's Healer,
keep me at even,
keep me at morning,
keep me at noon,
on rough course faring,
Help and safeguard
my means this night.
I am tired, astray, and stumbling,
shield thou me from snare and sin. AMEN.

(Carmina Gadelica)

'A TIME TO BREAK DOWN …'

*Now I will tell you what I am going to do to my vineyard: I
will take away its hedge, and it will be destroyed; I will break
down its wall, and it will be trampled.*

~ Isaiah 5:5 ~

Meditation

Blessing in covenant Your chosen,
O God,
You gave them all they needed.
Then You waited
for the first fruits of faithfulness …

But disappointment was Your harvest.

You tore down
the wealth-protecting hedges of the rich.
You broke down
the walls that kept the poor outside.

Blessing in covenant the world
O God
You gave Yourself in Jesus
the choice vine
and He was all we needed.
Then You waited
for the first fruits of faithfulness …

We disappointed:
Jesus did not.

Though hedges and walls remain,
You have taught us, Jesus,
that we cannot hedge ourselves in
for comfort, or apartness or holiness.
And Your Spirit's power
breaks down the walls
that separate one from another
in the universal language of love
that feeds the fruits of faithfulness.

Prayer

Dear Lord,
bless Your church.
Help us be open and hospitable.
Send us out to rejoice and to serve.
Tear down the hedges
that divide denominations and parishes.
Break down the walls
that exclude or confuse.
And keep us faithful we pray
to the essence of Christ
in whom there is
no separation of race,
nor gender or sexuality,
nor class or caste –
simply
one body of love. AMEN.

Suggested Scripture Readings

Isaiah 5:1–7   *'The parable of the vineyard'*
Psalm 28   *'The Lord breaks down what is evil'*

Prayers for Others

Pray for those who long to break down all that keeps
them captive. Pray for those who are having a break down
– spiritually, mentally or physically. Bless those who break
down harmful barriers and help to build others up.

Blessing

May you remain rooted in God,
grafted to the vine of Christ
and open to the Holy Spirit
that You may be fruitful
in all you do and are. AMEN.

'A TIME TO BUILD UP …'

And I tell you that you are Peter, and on this rock I will build my church, and the gates of Hades will not overcome it.

~ Matthew 16:18 ~

Meditation

A builder confidently
constructs the walls.
The bricks all of regular size and dimension
stand proudly to the side
awaiting their careful and experienced placement
within the structure being put together.

The child
scatters the Lego across the floor
looking for just the right size piece
to finish the latest creation
born of imagination
and fashioned in the knowledge
that all pieces will connect together.

To build God's church with people:
that takes skill, craft and patience!
For no two people are the same,
and finding those that can
sit alongside each other with ease
is an inspiring process.
A task that has been described by some
as 'building with bananas'.

Despite the unusual building material
the house of God has firm foundations in Christ
and walls that accommodate
those of every size and shape,
varying talents and hopes,
diverse opinions and none,
the introvert and the extrovert,
with age and gender no barrier to being included.

Prayer

God of many names,
Your voice echoes into the world
naming the qualities and endeavours
that build and shape communities,
giving form to Your presence.
In a world where violence, greed,
poverty, apathy and anger
ebb away at confidence
hosted within Your community,
You call forth
love, hope, faith,
justice and mercy
trusting humanity with the gifts
that have been offered in Christ
and dispersed by Your Holy Spirit.
As we hear the names You speak
and the gifts they inspire from us
may we take confidence
from the belief
You have for Your creation. AMEN.

Suggested Scripture Readings

Matthew 16:13–20   *'Peter's confession of Christ'*
1 Peter 2:4–6   *'The Living Stone'*

Prayers for Others

Pray for unity in the church congregations and for a place
where all talents are recognised and welcome.

Blessing

May the Lord lift up your face,
as Christ calls your name,
and the Holy Spirit leads you
to explore your unacknowledged gifts. AMEN.

'A TIME TO WEEP ...'

Jesus turned and said to them, 'Daughters of Jerusalem, do not weep for me; weep for yourselves and for your children'.

~ Luke 23:28 ~

Meditation

In Scots there is a word
used for weeping –
'greetin''.
'Dinna greet',
a child might be told,
having fallen over and been up-righted.
While 'have a guid greet'
sounds like words spoken
to the lost love of adolescence;
or the recently bereaved;
or the family who face the impact of terminal illness.

'Greetin'' invites the sorrowful
to meet all the emotion of weeping,
and walk the anguished path of tears
that leads them to inhabit new worlds.

So in weeping
we 'greet' the remorse of all that is now past;
we 'greet' the pain of hurts received and offered;
we 'greet' the memories that ask us to adventure in life
    again.

Prayer

Today Lord,
there will be those
who weep for their situation
and for the situations of their loved ones,
their communities,
and our world.
As their tear-stained faces
bear the prayers
they could not find the words for,

may they move from all hopelessness
to find your comforting voice
calling them towards a resolution
yet to be discovered. AMEN.

Suggested Scripture Readings

> Luke 23:26–31   *'Jesus' journey to the cross'*
> Jeremiah 31:15–17   *'God offers comfort'*

Prayers for Others

Remember those who feel overwhelmed with sadness and
those who sit with them and weep with them.

Blessing

> Sometimes we sorrow, other times we embrace,
> sometimes we question everything we face;
> yet in our yearning is a deeper learning:
> we belong to God, we belong to God.
>
> (From *CH4* 726 verse 3 written by Roberto Escamilla)

'A TIME TO LAUGH …'

Sarah said, 'God has brought me laughter, and everyone who hears about this will laugh with me'.

~ Genesis 21:6 ~

Meditation

With a belly-aching roar
new life bursts through my veins.
The excitement of this moment
is to be shared beyond this time,
for when others hear the story
they too will laugh
at the impossibility of this.

With a tentative titter
remember the disbelief
that the Lord wandered through.
It couldn't be me
that he thought he could use
to bring his plan to birth.
So many reasons to offer,
hoping that escape could be made.

With ripples of relief
this laughter accepts the transformation
of my life:
of God's intending purpose.

Prayer

In our human existence,
You, God of merriment,
are dancing in the ridiculous
so that I might catch a glimpse.
For laughter speaks of the amusing moments of life;
and of the uncomfortable when I am uncertain.
I thank you
that with friends and family
laughter builds up our relationships.
And I thank you that some laughter

can teasingly disarm my faults and flaws,
issuing an invitation to follow a different path.
Humour me, laughing God. AMEN.

Suggested Scripture Readings

Genesis 21:1–6   *'The birth of Isaac'*
Psalm 126:1–6   *'A song of joy'*

Prayers for Others

Pray for all of those who help the church become a place
of laughter, and remember all of those who help us laugh at
our own pretentions.

Blessing

May the laughter of God
ripple over my spirit
and allow me to encounter
the humour of daily living. AMEN.

'A TIME TO MOURN ...'

*Then they sat on the ground with him for seven days and
seven nights. No one said a word to him, because they saw
how great his suffering was.*

~ Job 2:13 ~

Meditation

After all this time
it feels wrong that I should still mourn.

Some days I say, 'Pull yourself together!
The time to mourn is over. Move on!'

Some days I say, 'Where is your faith?
Is God's love not enough for you?
No need to mourn.
Be glad in his presence'.

But the truth is, the wound in my heart
has not yet healed.
So, held by him, I give myself to mourning –
to grief –
to weeping –
until the time to mourn
has passed
for now.

Prayer

Lord,
the wound of loss is raw
and the future seems desolate.
Where is my purpose now?

But you are the one
who suffered most, in all of history.
And so you sit with me
in the ashes of my faith.
You hold on to me,
and there are no words.

As I lift my face
I see your light
breaking into my darkness,

Bringing your calm, your healing, your hope.
And I will yet praise you,
my Savour and my God.
In Jesus' name. AMEN.

Suggested Scripture Readings

Job 2:1–13   *'Job's suffering'*
Psalm 42   *'Longing for God's help in distress'*

Prayers for Others

Remember those who are grieving the loss of someone or
something dear to them.

Blessing

Lord, let your Spirit meet us here
To mend the body, mind and soul,
And disentangle peace from pain
And make your broken people whole. AMEN.

(John L. Bell and Graham Maule)

'A TIME TO DANCE …'

Meanwhile, the older son was in the field. When he came near the house, he heard music and dancing. So he called one of the servants and asked him what was going on.

~ Luke 15:25–6 ~

Meditation

When a parent's heart is broken
but their child returns their laughter –
that is a time to dance.

When the young follow dreams
but come home to sing their tale –
that is a time to dance.

When love breaks all our rules,
and sings along with faith –
that is a time to dance.

When those who stand at the door
find themselves drawn in –
that is a time to dance.

When the food is shared among us,
and there is space at the table for all –
that is a time to dance.

When the trumpet calls and the dead rise,
And the heavenly banquet begins –
that is a time to dance.

Prayer

You, Lord God, made it all in your image.
The music, the dance and the dancers.

All three,
distinct, together, one.
Free and random movement,
jigs and reels,
pirouettes and spins

head-banging, foot stomping
and comedy dad-dancing.

On polished ballroom floors;
in festival tents and barns;
to the sounds of drum and bass,
pipe and chanter,
stadium chants
and songs of protest.

Each an invitation from you,
to take the place of stillness by the hand,
and let it find movement and shape.

Word made flesh
to dwell,
and dance
among us. AMEN.

Suggested Scripture Readings

Luke 15:11–32 *'The Prodigal Son'*
Jeremiah 31:10–14 *'Mourning into dancing'*

Prayers for Others

Remember those who cannot find their joy and give thanks
for those who cannot contain theirs.

Blessing

Dance and sing all the Earth,
gracious is that hand that tends you.
Love and care, everywhere
God with purpose send you.

(John L. Bell and Graham Maule)

'A TIME TO THROW AWAY STONES …'

*When they kept on questioning him, he straightened up and
said to them, 'If any one of you is without sin, let him be the
first to throw a stone at her'.*

~ John 8:7 ~

Meditation

Hard words
cast in condemnation
hung
as if suspended in the air.
Until, in a moment,
like stones they dropped
heavy
to the ground.

And in their place
there rose the lightest
sound of love
scattering
like smooth new pebbles
in the sand,
shaping
soft words of life.
And truth
turned heads.
And caution
was thrown to the wind.
And fear
was flung to the furthest
corners of the earth.

And love remained.

Prayer

From your mouth, Lord,
words of love come tumbling among us.
From your arms
hope scatters in rock-hard places.

In your presence
a promise settles and makes its home.
Help us, Lord, to let go
of all that weighs us down this day;
to fling aside the hurts
we project at others
and to spread with joy
the love, the hope, the promise
you freely offer.
Make us ready
to throw in our lot with you.
In Jesus' name we pray. AMEN.

Suggested Scripture Readings

John 8:1–11   *'The woman caught in adultery'*
Joshua 4:1–7   *'Signs of God's presence'*

Prayers for Others

Pray for those who find it hard to let go of the past, who
need to lay it down that they might embrace the future.

Blessing

Stones guide the way.
Stones show the place.
Stones are the living signs
of promises made.
Bless the way we go,
bless the places we are,
bless the hopes we share, Lord,
that we might spread your truth
like pebbles in the sand. AMEN.

'A TIME TO GATHER STONES …'

The stone the builders rejected has become the capstone.

~ Psalm 118:22 ~

Meditation

Gathering stones …
To what purpose?
Laying foundations?
Building a home? A tower? Or a wall?
Or to be ready and armed?
Or, gathering stones with many, to lay a cairn, on the
    mountaintop?

Or, another reason:
gathering stones, with others, and leaving them
at a grave
to honour the dead with a visit
as is the Jewish custom?

Which will I choose?
perhaps that depends –
on the day –
and the time.

Prayer

Lord,
through the ages we have gathered stones.
We have used them to create.
We have built with them,
dwellings, cities, towers – for our protection.
Memorials – for remembrance.
temples and cathedrals – for your glory.

And we have used stones to destroy.
We have built walls, to keep out those who are not like us,
and dividing walls that split communities.
Forgive us, Lord.

Remind us that we, too, are like gathered stones.
Remind us that we are like living stones, to be built into a
    spiritual house,
and to become a holy priesthood,
for the sake of all creation.

Remind us that our foundation is the stone you have laid in
    Zion,
that chosen and precious cornerstone,
that stumbling stone,
that capstone,
in whose name we come to you.

And remind us that without that stone
nothing we build can stand. AMEN.

Suggested Scripture Readings

Psalm 118   *'God's cornerstone'*
1 Peter 2:4–8   *'The living stones'*

Prayers for Others

Remember the people like you, whom you stand alongside,
whom God is building the church with.

Blessing

May you gather in Christ's name,
to be built up in him
and stand firm in his strength
for his glory and praise. AMEN.

CHRONOS AND KAIROS

You see, at just the right time (kairos), when we were still powerless, Christ died for the ungodly.

~ Romans 5:6 ~

Meditation

I have sat for *days*, Lord:
waiting for something I dreaded, or desperate for something
    to be over;
or longing for something to begin;
the clock on the wall, the watch on my wrist,
lying to me, that minutes only have gone by ...
Or the tick of the clock measuring hours,
where I had felt that moments only had passed.

Chronos. Time passing. Measured by a steady tick,
inflected by the hope, joy, fear that we inject,
but, whether plodding, skipping, trudging, racing by,
still *time passing ... And where, God, are you in this?*

Then, *sometimes*, even as it unfolds: a moment, a day,
a date on the calendar ... *an event* –
no clue, then, what it would contain, or mean,
sometimes, when it just *happened*, unannounced,
I look back, *and realise* ...
There was meaning there – and not of my making ...

Kairos. Event. Happening. Time-at-which ...
Time is in your hands, God; *chronos* and *kairos*.
Your hands – not the clock's – bending, plaiting, weaving –
bringing time together.
Time's own threads, with place, and people; things can
    happen!
Things happen, when the time was, is, shall be *right* ...

Prayer

Where God are You in all this?
You who are present in every second,
place, person and event.

You who are present
in every rainbow and ray of sun
in every joyous moment and global celebration:
in every earthquake and tsunami
in every tear, disaster and loss.
You who were present at the Cross and the Tomb.
Help me God of chronos and kairos
to find meaning in it all
to understand – even in part –
how this divine soap opera in which we act
in the end justifies its storylines through Jesus.

For I confess, Lord,
sometimes I cannot understand why
You do not act –
a moment in time when all is put right with the world.

Forgive me, Lord
for my metronome mentality.
Help me to keep time by Your Spirit,
to live in faith in chronos,
to glimpse the tiny kairos moments
in which You use me, and to wait in faith
until Your kairos comes for me. AMEN

Suggested Scripture Readings

 1 Corinthians 16:5–8   *'Pauls time in Corinth'*
 Romans 5:1–11   *'At just the right time'*

Prayers for Others

For those whose schedules are so busy that they struggle to
find time for love and life, in all its fullness.

Blessing

Blessed we are, when day by day,
our lives unfold out of God's love and grace.
blessed we are when the moment comes,
that we recognise God as *here, in this*. AMEN.

'A TIME TO EMBRACE ...'

Going at once to Jesus, Judas said, 'Greetings, Rabbi!' and kissed him. Jesus replied, 'Friend, do what you came for'.

~ Matthew 26:49–50 ~

Meditation

You who welcomed
outcasts with hugs and hopes;
who cuddled children
and gripped the hand
of the grieving;
under whose arms
an unsuspecting world
sought shelter,
you went on your way
the taste of a friend
still fresh on your lips,
the trace of his touch
the final familiarity.

A look of love and of longing;
a kiss of belief and of betrayal;
an embrace
which exposed the world,
held it for a second
and sealed its fate for all time.
One misguided moment
and all life would know
God's arms around it.

Prayer

Lord, there are times
when we hold you in our hearts
yet betray you with our lips;
when we embrace your word
yet release it unheard;
when we protect ourselves
at the expense of others.

May we, through your touch,
learn to love one another
without suspicion, without fear
without condemnation,
and hold one another as friends. AMEN.

Suggested Scripture Readings

Matthew 26:47–50   *'Judas betrays Jesus'*
Song of Solomon 2:6   *'A dream of love'*

Prayers for Others

Pray for those who are afraid to open themselves to up to others.

Blessing

May we know,
in the whisper of the breeze,
in the glance of a stranger,
in the touch of a friend,
God's embrace,
God's acceptance
and God's reassurance today and always. AMEN.

'A TIME TO REFRAIN FROM EMBRACING …'

If your brother sins against you, go and show him his fault, just between the two of you.

~ Matthew 18:15 ~

Meditation

A time may come when we can embrace again,
and our touch may show our intent.

Regret, forgiveness,
a fresh start.

But not now.
Now, a word must be spoken,
angers must be named,
and tears must be allowed to flow.
Now, we must stand apart,
joined as one, by this space between us.

Our space,
for holding our tensions,
for wrestling with our needs.
for grappling with our choices.
No holds barred.

A hard space, but a holy space,
one that we shall neither inhabit too long,
nor cross too early.

For in this space,
you become you, and I become me.
Named and known. Seen and heard.

Able to be embraced.

Prayer

Lord God,
I remain here, swaddled in silence and prayer.
Where everything is well with my soul.

And if all you had said was '*refrain from embracing*'
that would be fine.
Then I could remain here.

But here, in the quiet your question stirs –
'*What about the people you avoid?*'
and, the quiet waters become quickly muddied.

I'm not convinced God, you know what they are like.
What they say, what they do.
You know how I am grieved.
So here just now, caught between your counsels,
I ask for the time and space I need.
To learn forgiveness, to grow in grace,
that my heart would enlarge
to embrace them all
with the same love that you embrace me. AMEN.

Suggested Scripture Readings

Matthew 18:15–19   '*When someone sins against you*'
Romans 12:9–21   '*Bless and do not curse*'

Prayers for Others

For those working for reconciliation in the home, the
community or across the world.

Blessing

O God, enlarge my heart that it may be big enough
to receive the greatness of your love.
Stretch my heart that it may take into it
all those who with me around the world believe in Jesus.
Stretch it that it may take into it
all those who do not know him,
but who are my responsibility because I know him.
And stretch it that it may take in
all those who are not lovely in my eyes,
and whose hands I do not want to touch.
through Jesus Christ my Saviour. AMEN.

(African traditional)

'A TIME TO SEEK …'

My heart says of you, 'Seek his face!' Your face, Lord, I will
seek. Do not hide your face from me …'

~ Psalm 27:8–9a ~

Meditation

Like a new-born lover, I sought Your face.
I found it in stained glass windows,
in pulpit set-apart preachers,
in consecrated bread and wine,
and in the trusted words of sacred Scripture.
Then You hid Your face from me.

Like a faithful lover, I sought Your face again.
I found it in the face of Jesus
and the faces of Martin Luther King,
Mother Theresa, Nelson Mandela –
and other famous icons of Christ.
Then You hid Your face from me.

Like one bereaved, I sought Your face anew:
in family, friends and neighbours,
in the stranger at the bus stop,
in the beggar on the pavement,
in the drug addict I feared,
in the foreign war-ravaged child.
Then Love itself found me.
And I saw Your face everywhere.
My God,
what a range of expressions You have!

Prayer

Creator God,
so often we seek Your face in what we consider
to be the holy, the beautiful and the extraordinary.
So often we seek Your face
in our sorrows, our pains and our indecisions.
And so often –

we don't bother to seek Your face at all.
Contented with our lives
we just keep on keeping on.
Or faced with someone we don't like,
or find strange or scary or repulsive
we turn away.
Forgive us, God.
For when we stop seeking Your face
we may keep our 'I sight'.
But we lose our 'You sight'. AMEN.

Suggested Scripture Readings

Psalm 27   *'Song of confidence'*
Matthew 7:7–11   *'Seek and you will find'*

Prayers for Others

For those seeking God but never seeing, may they find hope
and a reason to keep watching and waiting. Pray for people
who are seeking companionship, or work, or a fresh start.

Blessing

Ask and it will be given to you.
Seek and you will find.
Knock and the door will be opened to you.
Lord bless our asking and our seeking.
And may we find ourselves
knocking at the right doors. AMEN.

'A TIME TO LOSE ...'

They all wept as they embraced him and kissed him. What grieved them most was his statement that they would never see his face again. Then they accompanied him to the ship.

~ Acts 20:37–8 ~

Meditation

Arms are empty,
hearts are hollow and words are lost,
in the leaving behind, in the letting go,
in the learning to live without.

Yet release can be
a lifted anchor
signalling a fresh start,
a new quest
for places to land
and safe haven for the soul.

Release can be
a vision reborn
through eyes clouded with tears,
as drops land on eager earth
ripe for the planting.

Release can be
a stepping from the tomb,
a folding away of grave clothes
and the unwrapping of a promise
warmed by the dawn.

And arms reach out
to embrace different dreams
hearts are filled
to overflowing
and words seek out the truth
in the leaving behind, in the letting go
in the learning to live again.

Prayer

None of us likes to let go, Lord:
of a loved one;
of a treasured memory;
of the safe places of the soul.
You told your friends,
that it was time to go
that goodbye was not farewell;
that this end was the beginning
of a new adventure
and that even unseen,
you were at and on their side.

Teach us, Lord, to release
all that holds us back
from letting go with you.
Remind us that believing can happen
without the need to see.
Show us that you have a hold on us
even when we leave go of you.
And may we know that in giving you our everything,
we have nothing to lose. AMEN.

Suggested Scripture Readings

Acts 20:36–8   *'Paul sets sail for Jerusalem'*
John 20:11–18   *'Jesus appears to Mary Magdalene'*

Prayers for Others

Pray for those dealing with losing something or someone
important in their lives.

Blessing

In the letting go
let there be love.
In the letting go
let there be hope.
In the letting go
let there be safe landing.
And in our losing
may we know God's finding us
and keeping us forever. AMEN.

'A TIME TO KEEP …'

But Mary treasured up all these things and pondered them in her heart.

~ Luke 2:19 ~

Meditation

Like Mary,
I sift the gold from the dross
of my memories
and hold fast
to that which is precious:
the whispered words of angels
in unexpected answers to prayer,
the epiphanies of grace
in the kindness of others,
the incarnations of love
in the ones who showed me Christ,
and the family and friends
who have been my home.
For I cannot keep hold of time itself –
it runs on towards a horizon
whose closeness I cannot gauge.
And even should I be robbed of mind
the treasures of my heart will still remain:
for love's anniversaries are wrapped in eternity
where all time begins and ends.

Prayer

Lord God,
You asked Your people Israel
to keep the Passover feast
as a time of remembering
their deliverance
from slavery to freedom.
Jesus,
You asked us to keep the Last Supper
as a time of remembering
our deliverance

from sin to forgiveness.
Holy Spirit,
You ask us to keep the day of Pentecost
as a time of remembering
our deliverance
from confusion to understanding.
Help us to remember always, Lord,
the things of faith that really matter:
the moments of transforming love
that keep us in Your image. AMEN.

Suggested Scripture Readings

Luke 2:8–20	*'The shepherds visit Mary'*
2 Chronicles 35:16–19	*'Keeping God's times'*

Prayers for Others

Pray for all who suffer from dementia and those who care
for them, for those who have suffered memory loss as a
result of injury or illness and for all who struggle to keep
their faith festivals and practices in the face of persecution.

Blessing

May the Lord bless you and keep you.
May the Lord make his face to shine upon you
and be gracious unto you.
May the Lord lift up his countenance upon you
and give you peace. AMEN.

'A TIME TO THROW AWAY …'

So they called to the blind man, 'Cheer up! On your feet!
He's calling you'. Throwing his cloak aside, he jumped to
his feet and came to Jesus.

~ Mark 10:49b–50 ~

Meditation

Aye, I seen it happen
and I think he must have left it by mistake.
I mean, he was half starved and half blind
and now he's half naked.
Why would he chuck away his jakeit like that?

It wisnae a trendy jakeit or anythin'
but if ye huvnae bought one,
and they catch ye begging,
they big Roman polis will chuck ye in a hole
and toss away the key.

No, he must have left it by mistake.
Mibe' he's got a new job
wi that bloke he was speaking with.
Though I cannae see what use a joiner has
for a old blind fella
that's just flung away his begging jakeit.

Though, I suppose if he isnae wearing it now
he's mibe' no a beggar anymore.

I wonder where he is now?

Prayer

I call out to you:
'Jesus, Son of David, have mercy on me!'
And again, I call out
'Son of David, Have mercy on me!'
Push past the crowd, Lord,
and drown out their words,
so I can hear your voice alone,

inviting me to a place
I've never dreamed of seeing.

Help me discard the security of this blanket,
the comfort it once offered has long worn thin.
Now it simply cloaks my vision,
dims my sight
and blinds me to the life you offer me.

Meet me in my first stumbling steps, Lord.
Uncloaked and unpretentious.
Guided by the sound of your word,
asking me the question:
'What do you want me to do for you?'

And when the fog starts to clear,
And my sight is gradually restored
help me find a way
of asking the same
of You. AMEN.

Suggested Scripture Readings

Mark 10:46–52   *'Blind Bartimaeus'*
Colossians 3:1–17   *'Holy living'*

Prayers for Others

For those people who provide education or employment
opportunities for those taking the first steps into a new life.

Blessing

O leave the things that let you down:
the lust for wealth or cheap renown,
the memory of what you've been,
the worst you've ever thought or seen.

And if you will go where I will go,
on pathways smooth and troublesome,
and if you will love as I will love,
You'll see on earth the kingdom come.

(John L. Bell and Graham Maule)

'A TIME TO TEAR …'

And when Jesus had cried out again in a loud voice, he gave up his spirit. At that moment the curtain of the temple was torn in two from top to bottom. The earth shook and the rocks split.

~ Matthew 27:50–1 ~

Meditation

My world has come to an end, but life around me goes on –
  relentlessly.
What I want is weeping and wailing and gnashing of teeth.
And the earth to shake and the rocks to split.
And the oceans to rise and the valleys to heave.
I want whirlwinds and hailstorms and thunder and
  lightning.
I want the earth to stop turning and the sun to lose its light.

I want ashes on heads and clothes to be ripped.

But all that happens is that life goes on –
and my heart is torn within me.

Where we live, we hide our pain.
Our suffering causes barely a ripple on the waters.
'Keep smiling', we're told, even when all inside is turmoil.
But at the death of the Son of God, the Father did not hide
  his pain.
He tore his clothes –
so we would see his tears.

And healing came –
for all the world.

Prayer

Lord,
there is so much suffering in our world.
By rights, no clothes should be left untorn.

Day by day in the news we hear of wars and rumours of
  wars.

We hear of disaster and mayhem and chaos.
To our shame we have learned to live with injustice,
with oppression, with cruelty and killing,
and we don't shout out enough.

And in our own lives, we often suffer in silence
because no-one has the time to listen and to care.

But that day, when Jesus breathed his last on Calvary,
you did not hide your grief.
The earth shook; there was darkness, and the curtain was
    torn
to reveal the holiest place – your very heart.

Teach us, Lord, how to shake the earth in our day,
how to make our grief known, and how to tear our clothes
    in pain –
until healing comes
to hearths and hearts, for Jesus' sake. AMEN.

Suggested Scripture Readings

Matthew 27:45–56   *'Jesus death rips into time'*
Job 1:1–22   *'Job tears his clothes'*

Prayers for Others

For those whose hopes and hearts are sundered, may
they find the support and the love of others until they are
restored.

Blessing

In your suffering, may you know the holy heart of God,
which is broken – and torn apart
for you –
so that healing may begin. AMEN.

'A TIME TO MEND …'

There is neither Jew nor Greek, slave nor free, male nor female, for you are all made one in Christ Jesus.

~ Galatians 3:28 ~

Meditation

How can they all be mended Lord?
The burst trousers
and wee skint knees that come home
after a game of British Bulldogs
on a grassy playing field.

How can they all be mended Lord?
The torn green or blue football shirts
and bruised faces that come home
after the beautiful game turned ugly
on a gravelly football field.

How can they all be mended Lord?
The communities torn apart
because a son will never come home
after religious strife played out
on a bloody battlefield.

Make us to be your 'menders' Lord,
tailors of truth and love,
especially where the edges are most frayed.

People who cherish the handiwork,
of the one who weaves life in the womb.
A close-knit community
drawn together from worlds apart,
stitched upon your banner that reads:

'Not in my name'.

Prayer

You came to earth, Lord Jesus,
holding within yourself
all that we are,

and all that we might become.
Showing us how to join together
people made of clashing colours,
and cut form different cloth.

Jew with Gentile,
male with female,
Catholic with Protestant,
us with them.

You stretched out your arms, Lord Jesus,
and as your body was broken
and your Father tore his temple cloth,
you pierced the fabric of heaven and earth,
threading them together as a seamless whole.
Mending the world and all its people,
for now and forever. AMEN.

Suggested Scripture Readings

| Galatians 3:28 | *'All are made one in Christ'* |
| Colossians 1:19–20 | *'Christ reconciling heaven and earth'* |

Prayers for Others

For those working against sectarianism and those promoting ecumenism. And for all those ordinary families living extraordinary lives of reconciliation amidst torn communities.

Blessing

> Good is stronger than evil;
> love is stronger than hate;
> light is stronger than darkness;
> life is stronger than death.
> Victory is ours, through him who loves us.

(Desmond Tutu)

'A TIME TO KEEP SILENCE …'

He was oppressed and afflicted, yet he did not open his mouth; he was led like a lamb to the slaughter, and as a sheep before her shearers is silent, so he did not open his mouth.

~ Isaiah 53:7 ~

Meditation

How easy it is to give as good as I get;
to give folk a piece of my mind;
to let them have it;
to tell it like (I think) it is,
to set the record straight.

But, the tongue is a fire …
setting on fire the whole course of life.
How much harder it is to hold back;
to keep my mouth shut;
to swallow my words.
How hard it is to remain 'shtumm'.

Friendships are ended with fast pronouncements.
Hearts are broken with hasty words.
And healing needs the intervention of heaven.

Prayer

Lord,
Your voice is heard in the sound of utter silence,
and with that silence you challenge us.
When we fill our world with babble, out of the fear of
    silence,
you break through to us
with the stillness of your peace.

Help us to learn when to hold our tongue –
for the sake of others – and for our own sake.
Help us to study silence;
to find our peace in it, and to make peace with it.

We pray in the name of the One who was silent,
who opened not his mouth, but whose truth is still shouted
from all the rooftops of the world. AMEN.

Suggested Scripture Readings

Isaiah 53:1–9   *'The suffering servant'*
James 3:1–12   *'Taming the tongue'*

Prayers for Others

Remember those who find silence daunting and who fill
each moment with chitter and chatter. May they know a
new stillness that leads to peace, and quiet.

Blessing

'Speech is of time,
Silence is of eternity'

(Thomas Carlyle)

In the storms and earthquakes and fires of daily living,
may the silence of God find you,
and give you peace,
time after time. AMEN.

'A TIME TO SPEAK …'

If I speak in the tongues of men and of angels, but have not love, I am only a resounding gong or a clanging cymbal.

~ 1 Corinthians 13:1 ~

Meditation

The isle is full of noises:
our cities, our towns and our homes
are filled to their gullets with
cars, helicopters, radios, televisions,
roadworks, music, muzak;
a continual round of sound and clatter.

Do we cherish the words of people amidst all this?
Do we know our own voice to be a gift to us
and a gift for others?
Do the words we choose
at the moments we choose to speak them,
delight and hurt not?
Do our writings, our speakings, our emails and our texts
work towards justice?
and the kingdom of Jesus here on earth?

Prayer

Father, I give thanks that just as a mother knows the cry of
    her baby
in a house full of noises,
so you know my voice as mine and mine alone –
its tone, its pitch, its timbre.
Let me use it to speak for the suppressed and outcast people
    of the world,
but also to speak to the lonely and difficult people of my
    community.
At work, at church, at parties, oh Lord,
give me the strength to do something out of the ordinary
to break away from my comfortable groups
and talk with those in need of company, friendship and
    conversation. AMEN.

Suggested Scripture Readings

1 Corinthians 13:1–13   *'Speak with love'*
Proverbs 31:8–9   *'Speak for the poor'*

Prayers for others

For everyone who gives time and energy to those who may
not be spoken to, joked with and comforted by many other
voices.

Blessing

May my shouts be for justice.
May my shouts be of praise.
May my shouts be for the joy
and thrill and honour of following you,
and living in your gloryfilled world,
among your lightfilled people. AMEN.

'A TIME TO LOVE …'

Many waters cannot quench love; rivers cannot wash it away.
~ Song of Solomon 8:7 ~

Meditation

If I have not love
the edges of my heart
grow numb and ragged
and my song is worth
nothing.

If I have not love
I turn from my neighbour
in his need
and the relationship falters
by the wayside.

If I have not love
my soul cannot shout
of the greatness
of surrendering myself
for others.

That day on a tree,
when hate burst forth
from festering hearts,
spitting nails and bile,
was the time
when love had every right
to walk away.

But this time
love turned to the world,
sang and shouted,
gave itself up
and never gave in.
This time
for all time
love became life.
And I have love.

Prayer

God of life,
when the time was right
you came in love.
When the time was right
you gave in love.
When the time was right
you threw open a tomb
and love walked into the world
to stay.

As long as we live in you
may we love in you.
As long as we love in you
may we live for one another.
And as long as we have life
may we seek to share it
in the loving way
of your Son, Jesus Christ,
in whose name we pray. AMEN.

Suggested Scripture Readings

Song of Solomon 8:7   *'The power of love'*
John 13:33–5   *'A new commandment'*

Prayers for Others

Pray with thanks for those who know love, and with hope
for those who feel unloved.

Blessing

May we be held in love,
cradled in love,
joined in love
and let go in love.
That love
may be our lesson
and our living
and our life. AMEN.

'A TIME TO HATE ...'

Love must be sincere. Hate what is evil; cling to what is good.

~ Romans 12:9 ~

Meditation

Hate can be a demon.
Possessed of it
I am eaten away
from the inside out.
To hate another
demands a passion
equalled only by love.
Yet love creates –
the lover and the loved.
While hate destroys –
only the hater.

But I am called to hate.
'Hate what is evil.'
Teach me Lord
to separate the sin from the sinner:
even when that sin
tests my forgiveness to its limits.
Or
even when the sinner
is someone I once loved.

Teach me, Lord,
to use my hatred
with a passion
for justice and love.

Prayer

Loving God,
equip us, we pray,
where hate exists
to dismember it.

Enable us to triumph over fears
and prejudices
about those who are different or distant.
Help us to hate what you hate
and to use hate as a force for good.

And bless, dear Lord,
those who are consumed
with the wrong kind of hatred.
May they be remembered in love. AMEN.

Suggested Scripture Readings

Romans 12:9–21   *'The marks of a true Christian'*
Proverbs 6:16–19   *'God's hatred of evil'*

Prayers for Others

Pray for those whose hate of others is based on fear,
ignorance, superstition, racism, homophobia or religion,
and for those in relationships where love has turned to hate.

Blessing

May God bless all your desires.
May you inherit Jesus' hatred of evil.
May you possess the Spirit's power
to hold you fast to what is good
and to make your love genuine. AMEN.

'A TIME FOR WAR ...'

*Beat your plowshares into swords and your pruning hooks
into spears. Let the weakling say, 'I am strong!'.*

~ Joel 3:10 ~

Meditation

I will fight
where fear and power
bloody battlefields and stain souls.

I will fight
where greed and abuse
starve stomachs and destroy dreams.

I will fight
where wrong declares it's right
where suffering holds sway
where words of war have the final say.

And I will be a mercy mercenary.
And good news will be my ammunition.
And love will be my weapon.
And grace will make me bullet-proof.

And weakness in its strength
will win the day again
because I will fight.

Prayer

We talk of just war
but just what is that?
We talk of peace-keeping
yet we keep seeing lives in pieces.
We talk of means to an end
but what do we mean?

For you, Lord, in a war-ravaged land,
justice was hands raised in comfort not conflict.
For you, peace was more than lack of hostility.

For you, the end came without a fight
yet death itself lay defeated.

Equip us, gracious God,
to confront the world's wrongs
and keep us fighting your corner. AMEN.

Suggested Scripture Readings

Joel 3:9–12	*'God sits in judgement'*
Matthew 5:38–45	*'Jesus says love your enemies'*

Prayers for Others

Pray for peace for the victims of war, wisdom for the
perpetrators of war and courage for those who serve in our
armed forces.

Blessing

Fight the good fight with all your might;
Christ is your strength, and Christ your right;
lay hold on life and it shall be
your joy and crown eternally.

(CH4 517)

'A TIME FOR PEACE …'

Go! I am sending you out like lambs among wolves. Do not take a purse or bag or sandals; and do not greet anyone on the road.

~ Luke 10:3–4 ~

Meditation

To our quiet town they came,
drumming in their doctrine
with the march of a thousand boots.

Into our homes they came
our doors are already unbarred
they have drilled us well.
To our food stores they came,
packing their greed on the backs of our sons.

To our meekness they came,
hands resting absently on swords now redundant.
As Caesar's face smirks from the single tiny coin,
given in mock-exchange.

No-one cries, no-one fights.
This is 'Pax Romana'
the peace of Rome upon us.

To our quiet homes they came.
Two tired travellers
unheard, unshod and unexpected.

Into our homes they came.
Blessing our welcome with stories and song.
To our food stores they came,
and when there was no bread
they shared in our hunger for justice
and thirst for peace.

To our meekness they came,
their empty hands joining ours
tilling soil and building on the earth
that one day we would inherit.

Everyone shares, all receive.
This is 'Pax Christi'
the peace of Christ among us.

Prayer

Lord God,
they went *out* and they went *without*.
without money or food, shoes or bags
and without a staff to defend themselves on the road.

Lord, I see the connection,
that empty-handed they could learn to rely on you.
That the lesson of less
is to learn of a treasure within.

Lord, talk to me about this in the quiet, please,
and show me where there are things that I hold onto
that are better left behind.

And in your patience and love,
help me begin to lay aside
the peace that the world has given,
so that my hands may be ready
to hold and to share the peace that you give. AMEN.

Suggested Scripture Readings

Luke 10:1–12   *'Soldiers of peace'*
Matthew 5:38–48   *'The road of non-violence'*

Prayers for Others

Remember all those whose radical life of peace inspires us
all to challenge acts of violence with acts of love.

Blessing

Come with me, come wander, come welcome the world.
Where strangers might smile, or where stone may be
    hurled.
Come leave what you cling to, lay down what you clutch,
and find with hands empty, that hearts can hold much.

(John L. Bell and Graham Maule)

OMEGA

He said to me: 'It is done. I am the Alpha and the Omega,
the Beginning and the End'.

~ Revelation 21:6 ~

Meditation

On this narrow bridge of time, Lord,
this 'now' between what-has-been and what-shall-be,
here I stand; before 'The Future', if I wanted to be
    grandiose!
Or, more humbly, just before 'what comes next … and after
    that …'
There are things I might do; things I can't – they're just not
    possibilities.
And things undreamt, unimaginable to me now.
And that's just me! *My story. Open and uncompleted …*

Is not this how it is with the whole, real world?
Branching, cascading possibilities, options, choices,
    decisions*: freedom.*
But also the decisions that choke off possibilities;
    captivity –
then *liberation*: the unimagined, unimaginable possibilities
    springing new
from stagnant situations, *culs-de-sac …*
Unimaginable billions of unfolding, open stories, expanding
    out of the past into the future …

How could there be a summing-up of all of this?
This universe –
how could its endless stories even be *told*?
What billions of trillions upon trillions of words – let alone
    one word –
could ever speak the meaning of all this?

Prayer

In Christ,
Your Word made flesh –
and this, Lord,

is our faith –
in him
who spoke Your being to the world,
in him
shall be spoken the world's stories,
when they are done;
spoken as Your story
with Your world –
in a word:
LOVE.
For the Word that was from the first with You, God –
Alpha,
shall be the Last Word.
Omega …
Amen Lord,
Let it be. AMEN.

Suggested Scripture Readings

Revelation 21:1–6a *'The new heaven and the new earth'*

1 Corinthians 15:21 –28 *'The resurrection of the dead'*

Prayers for Others

For those who have come to the end of a chapter, or the end of life itself. May they be fully at peace and ready for their journey onwards.

Blessing

God be in my head, and in my understanding
God be in my eyes and in my looking
God be in my mouth and in my speaking
God be in my heart and in my thinking
God be at my end, and at my departing.

Using *Pray Now* as a worship resource

Below is an example of how to take a day of *Pray Now* and augment it to produce a shorter act of communal worship. Essentially, all the sections can be used or just the leader's introduction followed by the Bible Reading, the Meditation, a short silence, the Prayer and the Blessing – this may be all that is required for opening devotions.

The service may be led by one voice or, instead, several voices may participate. Although the sections are read, the group may appreciate having individual copies of *Pray Now* to use during the service or to take away with them.

'A time to keep ...' (Day 21)

Leader   Our theme for worship together is 'A time to keep'.

We begin by listening to a reading from St Luke Chapter 2 verses 15–20. After hearing the angels' words, the shepherds make their way to Bethlehem.

Reading   Luke 2:15–20 (*or 8–20 if a longer reading is desired*)

Song   'Look forward in faith' (*CH4* 56: by Andrew Scobie, tune Cardross by Andrea A. Steele)

Leader   'But Mary treasured all these words and pondered them in her heart.'

What do we keep in our hearts? Listen now to this meditation. There will be a short silence afterwards for our own thoughts.

Meditation

Like Mary,
I sift the gold from the dross
of my memories
and hold fast
to that which is precious:
the whispered words of angels
in unexpected answers to prayer,

the epiphanies of grace
in the kindness of others,
the incarnations of love
in the ones who showed me Christ,
and the family and friends
who have been my home.
For I cannot keep hold of time itself –
it runs on towards a horizon
whose closeness I cannot gauge.
And even should I be robbed of mind
the treasures of my heart will still remain:
for love's anniversaries are wrapped in eternity
where all time begins and ends.

Silence (optional)

Reflection (optional)

Leader   What came out of that meditation for you?
Does anyone want to share their thoughts?

OR

Would anyone like to share one of their most
precious memories?
What happens to our most precious memories –
for they are unique to us – if we lose our capacity
to keep hold of them?

Prayer

Lord God,
You asked Your people Israel
to keep the Passover feast
as a time of remembering
their deliverance
from slavery to freedom.
Jesus,
You asked us to keep the Last Supper
as a time of remembering
our deliverance
from sin to forgiveness.
Holy Spirit,
You ask us to keep the day of Pentecost

as a time of remembering
our deliverance
from confusion to understanding.
Help us to remember always Lord,
the things of faith that really matter:
the moments of transforming love
that keep us in Your image. AMEN.

(NB if there are some present who may not understand the term 'Pentecost' then either explain it before the prayer or substitute 'the day when God sent You'. Also, there is a place here, if desired, for additional extempore prayers of thanksgiving and intercession.)

Blessing   May the Lord bless you and keep you.
            May the Lord make his face to shine upon you
            and be gracious unto you.
            May the Lord lift up His countenance upon you
            and give you peace. AMEN.

(NB this may be spoken by the leader, or another, or said together. Alternatively, if more singing is desired then *CH4* 786 'May the God of peace go with us, we travel from this place; may the love of Jesus keep us firm in hope an and full of grace' is also suitable. Words by Ian Jamieson to familiar tune 'Ae fond kiss'.)

Additional Resources

Hymns relevant to time suitable for various day titles:

'Lord for the years' (*CH4* 159)

'Praise to the Lord for the joys of the earth' (*CH4* 165)

'This is a day of new beginnings' (*CH4* 526)

'Lord of love and perfect wisdom' (*CH4* 702)

'When we are living in the Lord' (*CH4* 726)
(NB This hymn is particularly appropriate for a time to be born, to die, to weep, to embrace, to seek and to love, as all are mentioned.)

'In the bulb there is a flower' (*CH4* 727; especially relevant is verse 3)

There is also a wonderful hymn based on Psalm 31:15a. Being SM many tunes fit but it was notably sung to that wonderful Psalm tune 'Dennis' which is available on a Midi player or as an instrumental on YouTube; you may find it by simply searching for the tune on the internet. The words suggest that even if we are 'robbed of our minds' and cannot keep memories any more, our times are in God's hands and so our most precious memories are kept safe for us by God.

My times are in thy hand:
my Lord I wish them there;
my life, my friends, my soul I leave
entirely to thy care.

My times are in thy hand:
whatever they may be,
pleasing or painful, dark or bright,
as best may seem to thee.

My times are in thy hand:
why should I doubt or fear?
my Father's hand will never cause
His child a needless tear.

My times are in thy hand:
Jesus, the Crucified;
those hands my cruel sins had pierced
are now my guard and guide.

My times are in thy hand:
I'll always trust in thee;
and, after death, at thy right hand
I shall for ever be.

These words make a magnificent meditation or prayer in themselves, especially verses 1 and 3.

Pray Now 2012 Daily Lectionary

With regard to 'Festivals etc' that fall on weekdays we have restricted this to the ones mentioned in *Common Order*: St Andrew's Day, Christmas Day, Epiphany, Candlemas (Presentation of the Lord), Ash Wednesday, Holy Week (including Maundy Thursday, Good Friday and Holy Saturday), Ascension Day and All Saints' Day. For each of these we have given the readings from the Year B provision in *Common Order*.

Sunday 27 November
Isaiah 64:1–9
Psalm 80:1–8, 18–20
1 Corinthians 1:3–9
Mark 13:24–end

Monday 28 November
Isaiah 2:1–5
Psalm 122
Matthew 8:5–11

Tuesday 29 November
Isaiah 11:1–10
Psalm 72:1–4, 18–19
Luke 10:21–4

Wednesday 30 November
St Andrew's Day
Isaiah 52:7–10
Psalm 19:1–6
Romans 10:12–18
Matthew 4:18–22

Thursday 1 December
Isaiah 26:1–6
Psalm 118:18–27a
Matthew 7:21, 24–7

Friday 2 December
Isaiah 29:17–end
Psalm 27:1–4, 16–17
Matthew 9:27–31

Saturday 3 December
Isaiah 30:19–21, 23–6
Psalm 146:4–9
Matthew 9:35 — 10:1, 6–8

Sunday 4 December
Isaiah 40:1–11
Psalm 85:1–2, 8–13
2 Peter 3:8–15a
Mark 1:1–8

Monday 5 December
Isaiah 35
Psalm 85:7–end
Luke 5:17–26

Tuesday 6 December
Isaiah 40:1–11
Psalm 96:1, 10–end
Matthew 18:12–14

Wednesday 7 December
Isaiah 40:25–end
Psalm 103:8–13
Matthew 11:28–end

Thursday 8 December
Isaiah 41:13–20
Psalm 145:1, 8–13
Matthew 11:11–15

Friday 9 December
Isaiah 48:17–19
Psalm 1
Matthew 11:16–19

Saturday 10 December
2 Kings 2:9–12
Psalm 80:1–4, 18–19
Matthew 17:10–13

Sunday 11 December
Isaiah 61:1–4, 8–end
Psalm 126
1 Thessalonians 5:16–24
John 1:6–8, 19–28

Monday 12 December
Numbers 24:2–7, 15–17
Psalm 25:3–8
Matthew 21:23–7

Tuesday 13 December
Zephaniah 3:1–2, 9–13
Psalm 34:1–6, 21–2
Matthew 21:28–32

Wednesday 14 December
Isaiah 45:6b–8, 18, 21b–end
Psalm 85:7–end
Luke 7:18b–23

Thursday 15 December
Isaiah 54:1–10
Psalm 30:1–5, 11–end
Luke 7:24–30

Friday 16 December
Isaiah 56:1–3a, 6–8
Psalm 67
John 5:33–6

Saturday 17 December
Genesis 49:2, 8–10
Psalm 72:1–5, 18–19
Matthew 1:1–17

Sunday 18 December
2 Samuel 7:1–11, 16
Psalm 89:1–4, 19–26
Romans 16:25–end
Luke 1:26–38

Monday 19 December
Judges 13:2–7, 24–end
Psalm 71:3–8
Luke 1:5–25

Tuesday 20 December
Isaiah 7:10–14
Psalm 24:1–6
Luke 1:26–38

Wednesday 21 December
Zephaniah 3:14–18
Psalm 33:1–4, 11–12, 20–end
Luke 1:39–45

Thursday 22 December
1 Samuel 1:24–end
Psalm 113
Luke 1:46–56

Friday 23 December
Malachi 3:1–4, 4:5–end
Psalm 25:3–9
Luke 1:57–66

Saturday 24 December
Christmas Eve
2 Samuel 7:1–5, 8–11, 16
Psalm 89:2, 19–27
Acts 13:16–26
Luke 1:67–79

Sunday 25 December
Christmas Day
Isaiah 9:2–7
Psalm 96
Titus 2:11–14
Luke 2:1–20

Monday 26 December
2 Chronicles 24:20–2
Psalm 119:161–8
Acts 7:51–end
Matthew 10:17–22

Tuesday 27 December
Exodus 33:7–11a
Psalm 117
1 John 1:1
John 21:19b–end

Wednesday 28 December
Jeremiah 31:15–17
Psalm 124
1 Corinthians 1:26–9
Matthew 2:13–18

Thursday 29 December
1 John 2:3–11
Psalm 96:1–4
Luke 2:22–35

Friday 30 December
1 John 2:12–17
Psalm 96:7–10
Luke 2:36–40

Saturday 31 December
1 John 2:18–21
Psalm 96:1, 11–end
John 1:1–18

Sunday 1 January
Numbers 6:22–end
Psalm 8
Genesis 17:1–13

Galatians 4:4–7
Luke 2:15–21

Monday 2 January
1 John 2:22–8
Psalm 98:1–4
John 1:19–28

Tuesday 3 January
1 John 2:29—3:6
Psalm 98:2–7
John 1:29–34

Wednesday 4 January
1 John 3:7–10
Psalm 98:1, 8–end
John 1:35–42

Thursday 5 January
1 John 3:11–21
Psalm 100
John 1:43–end

Friday 6 January
Epiphany of the Lord
Isaiah 60:1–6
Psalm 72:1–7, 10–14
Ephesians 3:1–12
Matthew 2:1–12

Saturday 7 January
1 John 3:22—4:6
Psalm 2:7–end
Matthew 4:12–17, 23–end

Sunday 8 January
Genesis 1:1–5
Psalm 29
Acts 19:1–7
Mark 1:4–11

Monday 9 January
1 Samuel 1:1–8
Psalm 116:10–15
Mark 1:14–20

Tuesday 10 January
1 Samuel 1:9–20
1 Samuel 2:1, 4–8
Mark 1:21–8

Wednesday 11 January
1 Samuel 3:1–10, 19–20
Psalm 40:1–4, 7–10
Mark 1:29–39

Thursday 12 January
1 Samuel 4:1–11
Psalm 44:10–15, 24–5
Mark 1:40–end

Friday 13 January
1 Samuel 8:4–7, 10–end
Psalm 89:15–18
Mark 2:1–12

Saturday 14 January
1 Samuel 9:1–4, 17–19, 10:1*a*
Psalm 21:1–6
Mark 2:13–17

Sunday 15 January
1 Samuel 3:1–20
Psalm 139:1–5, 12–18
1 Corinthians 6:11–end
John 1:43–end

Monday 16 January
1 Samuel 15:16–23
Psalm 50:8–24
Mark 2:18–22

Tuesday 17 January
1 Samuel 16:1–13
Psalm 89:19–27
Mark 2:23–end

Wednesday 18 January
1 Samuel 17:32–3, 37, 40–51
Psalm 144:1–2, 9–10
Mark 3:1–6

Thursday 19 January
1 Samuel 18:6–9, 19:1–7
Psalm 56:1–2, 8–end
Mark 3:7–12

Friday 20 January
1 Samuel 24:3–22*a*
Psalm 57:1–2, 8–end
Mark 3:13–19

Saturday 21 January
2 Samuel 1:1–4, 11–12, 17–19,
    23–end
Psalm 80:1–6
Mark 3:20–1
Matthew 25:31–end

Sunday 22 January
Jonah 3:1–5, 10
Psalm 62:5–12

1 Corinthians 7:29–31
Mark 1:14–20

Monday 23 January
2 Samuel 5:1–7, 10
Psalm 89:19–27
Mark 3:22–30

Tuesday 24 January
2 Samuel 6:12–15, 17–19
Psalm 24:7–end
Mark 3:31–end

Wednesday 25 January
Jeremiah 1:4–10
Psalm 67
Acts 9:1–22
Matthew 19:27–end

Thursday 26 January
2 Samuel 7:18–19, 24–end
Psalm 132:1–5, 11–15
Mark 4:21–5

Friday 27 January
2 Samuel 11:1–10, 13–17
Psalm 51:1–6, 9
Mark 4:26–34

Saturday 28 January
2 Samuel 12:1–7, 10–17
Psalm 51:11–16
Mark 4:35–end

Sunday 29 January
Deuteronomy 18:15–20
Psalm 111
Revelation 12:1–5*a*
Mark 1:21–8

Monday 30 January
2 Samuel 15:13–14, 30, 16:5–13
Psalm 3
Mark 5:1–20

Tuesday 31 January
2 Samuel 18:9–10, 14, 24–5,
    30 — 19:3
Psalm 86:1–6
Mark 5:21–end

Wednesday 1 February
2 Samuel 24:2, 9–17
Psalm 32:1–8
Mark 6:1–6*a*

Thursday 2 February
Presentation of the Lord
Malachi 3:1–5 *MP*
Psalm 24
Hebrews 2:14–end
Luke 2:22–40

Friday 3 February
Psalm 17 and 19
Psalm 18:31–6, 50–end
Mark 6:14–29

Saturday 4 February
1 Kings 3:4–13
Psalm 119:9–16
Mark 6:30–4

Sunday 5 February
Isaiah 40:21–end
Psalm 147:1–12, 20 and 21*c*
1 Corinthians 9:16–23
Mark 1:29–39

Monday 6 February
1 Kings 8:1–7; 9–13
Psalm 132:1–9
Mark 6:53–end

Tuesday 7 February
1 Kings 8:22–3, 27–30
Psalm 84:1–10
Mark 7:1–13

Wednesday 8 February
1 Kings 10:1–10
Psalm 37:3–6, 30–2
Mark 7:14–23

Thursday 9 February
1 Kings 11:4–13
Psalm 106:3, 35–41
Mark 7:24–30

Friday 10 February
1 Kings 11:29–32, 12:19
Psalm 81:8–14
Mark 7:31–end

Saturday 11 February
1 Kings 12:26–32, 13:33–end
Psalm 106:6–7, 20–3
Mark 8:1–10

Sunday 12 February
Proverbs 8:1, 22–31
Psalm 104:26–end
Colossians 1:15–20
John 1:1–14

Monday 13 February
James 1:1–11
Psalm 119:65–72
Mark 8:11–13

Tuesday 14 February
James 1:12–18
Psalm 94:12–18
Mark 8:14–21

Wednesday 15 February
James 1:19–end
Psalm 15
Mark 8:22–6

Thursday 16 February
James 2:1–9
Psalm 34:1–7
Mark 8:27–33

Friday 17 February
James 2:14–24, 26
Psalm 112
Mark 8:34—9:1

Saturday 18 February
James 3:1–10
Psalm 12:1–7
Mark 9:2–13

Sunday 19 February
The Transfiguration
2 Kings 2:1–12
Psalm 50:1–6
2 Corinthians 4:3–6
Mark 9:2–9

Monday 20 February
James 3:13–end
Psalm 19:7–end
Mark 9:14–29

Tuesday 21 February
James 4:1–10
Psalm 55:7–9, 24
Mark 9:30–7

Wednesday 22 February
Ash Wednesday
Joel 2:1–2, 12–17
Psalm 51:1–18
2 Corinthians 5:20b—6:10
Matthew 6:1–6, 16–21

Thursday 23 February
Deuteronomy 30:15–end
Psalm 1
Luke 9:22–5

Friday 24 February
Isaiah 58:1–9a
Psalm 51:1–5, 17–18
Matthew 9:14–15

Saturday 25 February
Isaiah 58:9b–end
Psalm 86:1–7
Luke 5:27–32

Sunday 26 February
Genesis 9:8–17
Psalm 25:1–9
1 Peter 3:18–end
Mark 1:9–15

Monday 27 February
Leviticus 19:1–2, 11–18
Psalm 19:7–end
Matthew 25:31–end

Tuesday 28 February
Isaiah 55:10–11
Psalm 34:4–6, 21–2
Matthew 6:7–15

Wednesday 29 February
Jonah 3
Psalm 51:1–5, 17–18
Luke 11:29–32

Thursday 1 March
Esther 14:1–5, 12–14
Psalm 138
Matthew 7:7–12

Friday 2 March
Ezekiel 18:21–8
Psalm 130
Matthew 5:20–6

Saturday 3 March
Deuteronomy 26:16–end
Psalm 119:1–8
Matthew 5:43–end

Sunday 4 March
Genesis 17:1–7, 15–16
Psalm 22:23–end
Romans 4:13–end

Monday 5 March
Daniel 9:4–10
Psalm 79:8–14
Luke 6:36–8

Tuesday 6 March
Isaiah 1:10, 16–20
Psalm 50:8, 16–end
Matthew 23:1–12

Wednesday 7 March
Jeremiah 18:18–20
Psalm 31:4–5, 14–18
Matthew 20:17–28

Thursday 8 March
Jeremiah 17:5–10
Psalm 1
Luke 16:19–end

Friday 9 March
Genesis 37:3–4, 12–13, 17–28
Psalm 105:16–22
Matthew 21:33–43, 45–6

Saturday 10 March
Micah 7:14–15, 18–20
Psalm 103:1–4, 9–12
Luke 15:1–3, 11–end

Sunday 11 March
Exodus 20:1–17
Psalm 19 [19:7–end]
1 Corinthians 1:18–25
John 2:13–22

Monday 12 March
2 Kings 5:1–15
Psalms 42:1–2, 43:1–4
Luke 4:24–30

Tuesday 13 March
Daniel 2:20–3
Psalm 25:3–10
Matthew 18:21–end

Wednesday 14 March
Deuteronomy 4:1, 5–9
Psalm 147:13–end
Matthew 5:17–19

Thursday 15 March
Jeremiah 7:23–8
Psalm 95:1–2, 6–end
Luke 11:14–23

Friday 16 March
Hosea 14
Psalm 81:6–10, 13, 16
Mark 12:28–34

Saturday 17 March
Hosea 5:15 — 6:6
Psalm 51:1–2, 17–end
Luke 18:9–14

Sunday 18 March
Numbers 21:4–9
Psalm 107:1–3, 17–22
Ephesians 2:1–10
John 3:14–21

Monday 19 March
2 Samuel 7:4–16
Psalm 89:26–36
Romans 4:13–18
Matthew 1:18–end

Tuesday 20 March
Ezekiel 47:1–9, 12
Psalm 46:1–8
John 5:1–3, 5–16

Wednesday 21 March
Isaiah 49:8–15
Psalm 145:8–18
John 5:17–30

Thursday 22 March
Exodus 32:7–14
Psalm 106:19–23
John 5:31–end

Friday 23 March
Jeremiah 26:8–11
Psalm 34:15–end
John 7:1–2, 10, 25–30

Saturday 24 March
Jeremiah 11:18–20
Psalm 7:1–2, 8–10
John 7:40–52

Sunday 25 March
Jeremiah 31:31–4
Psalm 51:1–13
Hebrews 5:5–10
John 12:20–33

Monday 26 March
Isaiah 7:10–14
Psalm 40:5–11
Hebrews 10:4–10
Luke 1:26–38

Tuesday 27 March
Numbers 21:4–9
Psalm 102:1–3, 16–23
John 8:21–30

Wednesday 28 March
Daniel 3:14–20, 24–5, 28
Psalm 55
John 8:31–42

Thursday 29 March
Genesis 17:3–9
Psalm 105:4–9
John 8:51–end

Friday 30 March
Jeremiah 20:10–13
Psalm 18:1–6
John 10:31–end

Saturday 31 March
Ezekiel 37:21–8
Jeremiah 31:10–13
John 11:45–end

HOLY WEEK

Sunday 1 April
Palm Sunday
Mark 11:1–11
Psalm 118:1–2, 19–29

Passion Sunday
Isaiah 50:4–9*a*
Psalm 31:9–16
Philippians 2:5–11
Mark 14:1–end of 15

Monday 2 April
Isaiah 42:1–9
Psalm 36:5–11
Hebrews 9:11–15
John 12:1–11

Tuesday 3 April
Isaiah 49:1–7
Psalm 71:1–14
1 Corinthians 1:18–31
John 12:20–36

Wednesday 4 April
Isaiah 50:4–9*a*
Psalm 70
Hebrews 12:1–3
John 13:21–32

Thursday 5 April
Maundy Thursday
Exodus 12:1–4 [5–10] 11–14
Psalm 116:1–end
1 Corinthians 11:23–6
John 13:1–17, 31*b*–35

Friday 6 April
Good Friday
Isaiah 52:13–end
Psalm 22
Hebrews 10:16–25
John 18:1–end

Saturday 7 April
Job 14:1–14
Psalm 31:1–4, 15–16
1 Peter 4:1–8
Matthew 27:57–end

Sunday 8 April
Easter Day
Acts 10:34–43 †
Psalm 118:1–2, 14–24
1 Corinthians 15:1–11
John 20:1–18

Monday 9 April
Acts 2:14, 22–32
Psalm 16:1–2; 6–end
Matthew 28:8–15

Tuesday 10 April
Acts 2:36–41
Psalm 33:4–5, 18–end
John 20:11–18

Wednesday 11 April
Acts 3:1–10
Psalm 105:1–9
Luke 24:13–35

Thursday 12 April

Acts 3:11–end
Psalm 8
Luke 24:35–48

Friday 13 April

Acts 4:1–12
Psalm 118:1–4, 22–6
John 21:1–14

Saturday 14 April

Acts 4:13–21
Psalm 118:1–4, 14–21
Mark 16:9–15

Sunday 15 April

Acts 4:32–5
Psalm 133
1 John 1:1—2:2
John 20:19–end

Monday 16 April

Acts 4:23–31
Psalm 2:1–9
John 3:1–8

Tuesday 17 April

Acts 4:32–end
Psalm 93
John 3:7–15

Wednesday 18 April

Acts 5:17–26
Psalm 34:1–8
John 3:16–21

Thursday 19 April

Acts 5:27–33
Psalm 34:1, 15–end
John 3:31–end

Friday 20 April

Acts 5:34–42
Psalm 27:1–5, 16–17
John 6:1–15

Saturday 21 April

Acts 6:1–7
Psalm 33:1–5, 18–19
John 6:16–21

Sunday 22 April

Acts 3:12–19
Psalm 4
1 John 3:1–7
Luke 24:36b–48

Monday 23 April

Revelation 12:7–12
Psalm 126
2 Timothy 2:3–13
John 15:18–21

Tuesday 24 April

Acts 7:51—8:1a
Psalm 31:1–5, 16
John 6:30–5

Wednesday 25 April

Proverbs 15:28–end
Psalm 119:9–16
Ephesians 4:7–16
Mark 13:5–13

Thursday 26 April

Acts 8:26–end
Psalm 66:7–8, 14–end
John 6:44–51

Friday 27 April

Acts 9:1–20
Psalm 117
John 6:52–9

Saturday 28 April

Acts 9:31–42
Psalm 116:10–15
John 6:60–9

Sunday 29 April

Acts 4:5–12
Psalm 23
1 John 3:16–end
John 10:11–18

Monday 30 April

Acts 11:1–18
Psalms 42:1–2, 43:1–4
John 10:1–10

Tuesday 1 May

Isaiah 30:15–21
Psalm 119:1–8
Ephesians 1:3–10
John 14:1–14

Wednesday 2 May

Acts 12:24—13:5
Psalm 67
John 12:44–end

Thursday 3 May

Acts 13:13–25
Psalm 89:1–2, 20–6
John 13:16–20

Friday 4 May

Acts 13:26–33
Psalm 2
John 14:1–6

Saturday 5 May

Acts 13:44–end
Psalm 98:1–5
John 14:7–14

Sunday 6 May

Acts 8:26–end
Psalm 22:25–end
1 John 4:7–end
John 15:1–8

Monday 7 May

Acts 14:5–18
Psalm 118:1–3, 14–15
Deuteronomy 16:1–20
John 14:21–6

Tuesday 8 May

Acts 14:19–end
Psalm 145:10–end
John 14:27–end

Wednesday 9 May

Acts 15:1–6
Psalm 122:1–5
John 15:1–8
1 Peter 2:1–10

Thursday 10 May

Acts 15:7–21
Psalm 96:1–3, 7–10
John 15:9–11

Friday 11 May

Acts 15:22–31
Psalm 57:8–end
John 15:12–17

Saturday 12 May

Acts 16:1–10
Psalm 100
John 15:18–21

Sunday 13 May

Acts 10:44–end
Psalm 98
1 John 5:1–6
John 15:9–17

Monday 14 May

Isaiah 22:15–end
Psalm 15
Acts 1:15–end
John 15:9–17

Tuesday 15 May

Acts 16:22–34
Psalm 138
John 16:5–11
Luke 6:39–end

Wednesday 16 May

Acts 17:15, 22 — 18:1
Psalm 148:1–2, 11–end
John 16:12–15

Thursday 17 May

Ascension Day
Acts 1:1–11
Psalm 47
Ephesians 1:15–end
Luke 24:44–end

Friday 18 May

Acts 18:9–18
Psalm 47:1–6
John 16:20–3

Saturday 19 May

Acts 18:22–end
Psalm 47:1–2, 7–end
John 2:7–17

Sunday 20 May

Acts 1:15–17, 21–end
Psalm 1
1 John 5:9–13
John 17:6–19

Monday 21 May

Acts 19:1–8
Psalm 68:1–6
John 16:29–end

Tuesday 22 May

Acts 20:17–27
Psalm 68:9–10, 18–19
John 17:1–11

Wednesday 23 May
Acts 20:28–end
Psalm 68:27–8, 32–end
John 17:11–19

Thursday 24 May
Acts 22:30, 23:6–11
Psalm 16:1, 5–end
John 17:20–end

Friday 25 May
Acts 25:13–21
Psalm 103:1–2, 11–12, 19–20
John 21:15–19

Saturday 26 May
Acts 28:16–20, 30–end
Psalm 11:4–end
John 21:20–end

Sunday 27 May
Pentecost
Acts 2:1–21
Psalm 104:26–36, 37*b*
Romans 8:22–7
John 15:26–7; 16:4*b*–15

Monday 28 May
1 Peter 1:3–9
Psalm 111
Mark 10:17–27

Tuesday 29 May
1 Peter 1:10–16
Psalm 98:1–5
Mark 10:28–31

Wednesday 30 May
1 Peter 1:18–end
Psalm 147:13–end
Mark 10:32–45

Thursday 31 May
Zephaniah 3:14–18
Psalm 113
Romans 12:9–16
Luke 1:39–56

Friday 1 June
1 Peter 4:7–13
Psalm 96:10–end
Mark 11:11–26

Saturday 2 June
Jude 17, 20–end
Psalm 63:1–6
Mark 11:27–end

Sunday 3 June
Trinity Sunday
Isaiah 6:1–8
Psalm 29
Romans 8:12–17
John 3:1–17

Monday 4 June
2 Peter 1:2–7
Psalm 91:1–2, 14–end
Mark 12:1–12

Tuesday 5 June
2 Peter 3:11–end
Psalm 90:1–16
Mark 12:13–17

Wednesday 6 June
2 Timothy 1:1–3, 6–12
Psalm 123
Mark 12:18–27

Thursday 7 June
2 Timothy 2:8–15
Psalm 25:4–12
Mark 12:28–34

Friday 8 June
2 Timothy 3:10–end
Psalm 119:161–8
Mark 12:35–7

Saturday 9 June
2 Timothy 4:1–8
Psalm 71:7–16
Mark 12:38–end

Sunday 10 June
1 Samuel 8:4–15
Psalm 138
2 Corinthians 4:13 — 5:1
Mark 3:20–end

Monday 11 June
Job 29:11–16
Psalm 112
Acts 11:19–end
John 15:12–17

Tuesday 12 June
1 Kings 17:7–16
Psalm 4
Matthew 5:13–16

Wednesday 13 June
1 Kings 18:20–39
Psalm 16:1, 6–end
Matthew 5:17–19

Thursday 14 June
1 Kings 18:41–end
Psalm 65:8–end
Matthew 5:20–6

Friday 15 June
1 Kings 19:9, 11–16
Psalm 27:8–16
Matthew 5:27–32

Saturday 16 June
1 Kings 19:19–end
Psalm 16:1–7
Matthew 5:33–7

Sunday 17 June
1 Samuel 15:34 — 16:13
Psalm 20
2 Corinthians 5:6–17
Mark 4:26–34

Monday 18 June
1 Kings 21:1–16
Psalm 5:1–5
Matthew 5:38–42

Tuesday 19 June
1 Kings 21:17–end
Psalm 51:1–9
Matthew 5:43–end

Wednesday 20 June
2 Kings 2:1, 6–14
Psalm 31:21–end
Matthew 6:1–6, 16–18

Thursday 21 June
Isaiah 63:7–9
Psalm 97:1–8
Matthew 6:7–15

Friday 22 June
2 Kings 11:1–4, 9–18, 20
Psalm 132:1–5, 11–13
Matthew 6:19–23

Saturday 23 June
2 Chronicles 24:17–25
Psalm 89:25–33
Matthew 6:24–end

Sunday 24 June
1 Samuel 17:1–23, 32–49
Psalm 9:9–end
2 Corinthians 6:1–13
Mark 4:35–end

Monday 25 June
Isaiah 40:1–11
Psalm 85:7–end
Acts 13:14*b*–26
Luke 1:57–66, 80

Tuesday 26 June
2 Kings 19:9*b*–11, 14–21, 31–6
Psalm 48:1–2, 8–end
Matthew 7:6, 12–14

Wednesday 27 June
2 Kings 22:8–13, 23:1–3
Psalm 119:33–40
Matthew 7:15–20

Thursday 28 June
2 Kings 24:8–17
Psalm 79:1–9, 12
Matthew 7:21–end

Friday 29 June
Zechariah 4:1–6*a*,
Psalm 125
Acts 12:1–11
Matthew 16:13–19

Saturday 30 June
Lamentations 2:2, 10–14, 18–19
Psalm 74:1–3, 21–end
Matthew 8:5–17

Sunday 1 July
2 Samuel 1:1, 17–end
Psalm 130
2 Corinthians 8:7–end
Mark 5:21–end

Monday 2 July
Amos 2:6–10; 13–end
Psalm 50:16–23
Matthew 8:18–22

Tuesday 3 July
Habakkuk 2:1–4
Psalm 31:1–6
Ephesians 2:19–end
John 20:24–9

Wednesday 4 July
Amos 5:14–15, 21–4
Psalm 50:7–14
Matthew 8:28–end

Thursday 5 July
Amos 7:10–end
Psalm 19:7–10
Matthew 9:1–8

Friday 6 July
Amos 8:4–6, 9–12
Psalm 119:1–8
Matthew 9:9–13

Saturday 7 July
Amos 9:11–end
Psalm 85:8–end
Matthew 9:14–17

Sunday 8 July
2 Samuel 5:1–5, 9–10
Psalm 48
2 Corinthians 12:2–10
Mark 6:1–13

Monday 9 July
Hosea 2:14–16, 19–20
Psalm 145:2–9
Matthew 9:18–26

Tuesday 10 July
Hosea 8:4–7, 11–13
Psalm 103:8–12
Matthew 9:32–end

Wednesday 11 July
Hosea 10:1–3, 7–8, 12
Psalm 115:3–10
Matthew 10:1–7

Thursday 12 July
Hosea 11:1, 3–4, 8–9
Psalm 105:1–7
Matthew 10:7–15

Friday 13 July
Hosea 14:2–end
Psalm 80:1–7
Matthew 10:16–23

Saturday 14 July
Isaiah 6:1–8
Psalm 51:1–7
Matthew 10:24–33

Sunday 15 July
2 Samuel 6:1–5, 12b–19
Psalm 24
Ephesians 1:3–14
Mark 6:14–29

Monday 16 July
Isaiah 1:11–17
Psalm 50:7–15
Matthew 10:34—11:1

Tuesday 17 July
Isaiah 7:1–9
Psalm 48:1–7
Matthew 11:20–4

Wednesday 18 July
Isaiah 10:5–7, 13–16
Psalm 94:5–11
Matthew 11:25–7

Thursday 19 July
Isaiah 26:7–9, 16–19
Psalm 102:14–21
Matthew 11:28–end

Friday 20 July
Isaiah 38:1–6, 21–2
Psalm 32:1–8
Matthew 12:1–8

Saturday 21 July
Micah 2:1–5
Psalm 10:1–5a, 12
Matthew 12:14–21

Sunday 22 July
2 Samuel 7:1–14a
Psalm 89:20–37
Ephesians 2:11–end
Mark 6:30–4, 53–end

Monday 23 July
Song of Solomon 3:1–4
Psalm 42:1–10
2 Corinthians 5:14–17
John 20:1–2, 11–18

Tuesday 24 July
Micah 7:14–15, 18–20
Psalm 85:1–7
Matthew 12:46–end

Wednesday 25 July
Jeremiah 45:1–5
Psalm 126
Acts 11:27—12:2
Matthew 20:20–8

Thursday 26 July
Jeremiah 2:1–3; 7–8, 12–13
Psalm 36:5–10
Matthew 13:10–17

Friday 27 July
Jeremiah 3:14–17
Psalm 23
Matthew 13:18–23

Saturday 28 July
Jeremiah 7:1–11
Psalm 84:1–6
Matthew 13:24–30

Sunday 29 July
2 Samuel 11:1–15
Psalm 14
Ephesians 3:14–end
John 6:1–21

Monday 30 July
Jeremiah 13:1–11
Psalm 82
Matthew 13:31–5

Tuesday 31 July
Jeremiah 14:17–end
Psalm 79:8–end
Matthew 13:36–43

Wednesday 1 August
Jeremiah 15:10, 16–end
Psalm 59:1–4, 18–end
Matthew 13:44–6

Thursday 2 August
Jeremiah 18:1–6
Psalm 146:1–5
Matthew 13:47–53

Friday 3 August
Jeremiah 26:1–9
Psalm 69:4–10
Matthew 13:54–end

Saturday 4 August
Jeremiah 26:11–16, 24
Psalm 69:14–20
Matthew 14:1–12

Sunday 5 August
2 Samuel 11:26—12:13a
Psalm 51:1–13
Ephesians 4:1–16
John 6:24–35

Monday 6 August
Daniel 7:9–10, 13–14
Psalm 97
2 Peter 1:16–19
Luke 9:28–36

Tuesday 7 August
Jeremiah 30:1–2, 12–15, 18–22
Psalm 102:16–21
Matthew 14:22–end

Wednesday 8 August
Jeremiah 31:1–7
Psalm 121
Matthew 15:21–8

Thursday 9 August
Jeremiah 31:31–4
Psalm 51:11–18
Matthew 16:13–23

Friday 10 August
Nahum 2:1, 3; 3:1–3, 6–7
Psalm 137:1–6
Matthew 16:24–8

Saturday 11 August
Habakkuk 1:12—2:4
Psalm 9:7–11
Matthew 17:14–20

Sunday 12 August
2 Samuel 18:5–9
Psalm 130
Ephesians 4:25 — 5:2
John 6:35, 41–51

Monday 13 August
Ezekiel 1:2–5, 24–end
Psalm 148:1–4, 12–13
Matthew 17:22–end

Tuesday 14 August
Ezekiel 2:8 — 3:4
Psalm 119:65–72
Matthew 18:1–5, 10, 12–14

Wednesday 15 August
Isaiah 61:10–end
Psalm 45:10–end
Galatians 4:4–7
Luke 1:46–55

Thursday 16 August
Ezekiel 12:1–12
Psalm 78:58–64
Matthew 18:21 — 19:1

Friday 17 August
Ezekiel 16:1–15, 60–end
Psalm 118:14–18
Matthew 19:3–12

Saturday 18 August
Ezekiel 18:1–11a, 13b, 30, 32
Psalm 51:1–3, 15–17
Matthew 19:13–15

Sunday 19 August
1 Kings 2:10–12; 3:3–14
Psalm 111
Ephesians 5:15–20
John 6:51–8

Monday 20 August
Ezekiel 24:15–24
Psalm 78:1–8
Matthew 19:16–22

Tuesday 21 August
Ezekiel 28:1–10
Psalm 107:1–3, 40, 43
Matthew 19:23–end

Wednesday 22 August
Ezekiel 34:1–11
Psalm 23
Matthew 20:1–16

Thursday 23 August
Ezekiel 36:23–8
Psalm 51:7–12
Matthew 22:1–14

Friday 24 August
Isaiah 43:8–13
Psalm 145:1–7
Acts 5:12–16
Luke 22:24–30

Saturday 25 August
Ezekiel 43:1–7
Psalm 85:7–end
Matthew 23:1–12

Sunday 26 August
1 Kings 8:1, 6, 10–11
Psalm 34:15–end
Ephesians 6:10–20
John 6:56–69

Monday 27 August
2 Thessalonians 1:1–5, 11–end
Psalm 39:1–9
Matthew 23:13–22

Tuesday 28 August
2 Thessalonians 2:1–3a, 14–end
Psalm 98
Matthew 23:23–6

Wednesday 29 August
2 Thessalonians 3:6–10, 16–end
Psalm 128
Matthew 23:27–32

Thursday 30 August
1 Corinthians 1:1–9
Psalm 145:1–7
Matthew 24:42–end

Friday 31 August
1 Corinthians 1:17–25
Psalm 33:6–12
Matthew 25:1–13

Saturday 1 September
1 Corinthians 1:26–end
Psalm 33:12–15, 20–end
Matthew 25:14–30

Sunday 2 September
Song of Solomon 2:8–13
Psalm 45:1–2, 6–9
James 1:17–end
Mark 7:1–8, 14–15, 21–3

Monday 3 September
1 Corinthians 2:1–5
Psalm 33:12–21
Luke 4:16–30

Tuesday 4 September
1 Corinthians 2:10*b*–end
Psalm 145:10–17
Luke 4:31–7

Wednesday 5 September
1 Corinthians 3:1–9
Psalm 62
Luke 4:38–end

Thursday 6 September
1 Corinthians 3:18–end
Psalm 24:1–6
Luke 5:1–11

Friday 7 September
1 Corinthians 4:1–5
Psalm 37:3–8
Luke 5:33–end

Saturday 8 September
1 Corinthians 4:6–15
Psalm 145:18–end
Luke 6:1–5

Sunday 9 September
Proverbs 22:1–2
Psalm 125
James 2:1–17
Mark 7:24–end

Monday 10 September
1 Corinthians 5:1–8
Psalm 5:5–9*a*
Luke 6:6–11

Tuesday 11 September
1 Corinthians 6:1–11
Psalm 149:1–5
Luke 6:12–19

Wednesday 12 September
1 Corinthians 7:25–31
Psalm 45:11–end 1
Luke 6:20–6

Thursday 13 September
1 Corinthians 8:1–7, 11–end
Psalm 139:1–9
Luke 6:27–38

Friday 14 September
Numbers 21:4–9
Psalm 22:23–8
Philippians 2:6–11
John 3:13–17

Saturday 15 September
1 Corinthians 10:14–22
Psalm 116:10–end
Luke 6:43–end

Sunday 16 September
Proverbs 1:20–33
Psalm 19:1–6
James 3:1–12
Mark 8:27–end

Monday 17 September
1 Corinthians 11:17–26, 33
Psalm 40:7–11
Luke 7:1–10

Tuesday 18 September
1 Corinthians 12:12–14, 27–end
Psalm 100
Luke 7:11–17

Wednesday 19 September
1 Corinthians 12:31b–end
Psalm 33:1–12
Luke 7:31–5

Thursday 20 September
1 Corinthians 15:1–11
Psalm 118:1–2, 17–20
Luke 7:36–end

Friday 21 September
Proverbs 3:13–18
Psalm 119:65–72
2 Corinthians 4:1–6
Matthew 9:9–13

Saturday 22 September
1 Corinthians 15:35–7, 42–9
Psalm 30:1–5
Luke 8:4–1

Sunday 23 September
Proverbs 31:10–end
Psalm 1
James 3:13 — 4:3, 7–8*a*
Mark 9:30–7

Monday 24 September
Proverbs 3:27–34
Psalm 15
Luke 8:16–18

Tuesday 25 September
Proverbs 21:1–6, 10–13
Psalm 119:1–8
Luke 8:19–21

Wednesday 26 September
Proverbs 30:5–9
Psalm 119:105–12
Luke 9:1–6

Thursday 27 September
Ecclesiastes 1:2–11
Psalm 90:1–6
Luke 9:7–9

Friday 28 September
Ecclesiastes 3:1–11
Psalm 144:1–4
Luke 9:18–22

Saturday 29 September
Genesis 28:10–17
Psalm 103:19–end
Revelation 12:7–12
John 1:47–end

Sunday 30 September
Esther 7:1–6, 9, 10
Psalm 124
James 5:13–end
Mark 9:38–end

Monday 1 October
Job 1:6–end
Psalm 17:1–11
1 Kings 21
Luke 9:46–50

Tuesday 2 October
Job 3:1–3, 11–17, 20–3
Psalm 88:14–19
Luke 9:51–6

Wednesday 3 October
Job 9:1–12, 14–16
Psalm 88:1–6, 11
Luke 9:57–end

Thursday 4 October
Job 19:21–7*a*
Psalm 27:13–16
Luke 10:1–12

Friday 5 October
Job 38:1, 12–21
Psalm 139:6–11
Luke 10:13–16

Saturday 6 October
Job 42:1–3, 6, 12–end
Psalm 119:169–end
Luke 10:17–24

Sunday 7 October
Job 1:1; 2:1–10
Psalm 26
Hebrews 1:1–4; 2:5–12
Mark 10:2–16

Monday 8 October
Galatians 1:6–12
Psalm 111:1–6
Luke 10:25–37

Tuesday 9 October
Galatians 1:13–end
Psalm 139:1–9
Luke 10:38–end

Wednesday 10 October
Galatians 2:1–2, 7–14
Psalm 117
Luke 11:1–4

Thursday 11 October
Galatians 3:1–5
Psalms 90, 92
Luke 11:5–13

Friday 12 October
Galatians 3:7–14
Psalm 111:4–end
Luke 11:15–26

Saturday 13 October
Galatians 3:22–end
Psalm 105:1–7
Luke 11:27–8

Sunday 14 October
Job 23:1–9, 16–end
Psalm 22:1–15
Hebrews 4:12–end
Mark 10:17–31

Monday 15 October
Galatians 4:21–4, 26–7, 31, 5:1
Psalm 113
Luke 11:29–32

Tuesday 16 October
Galatians 5:1–6
Psalm 119:41–8
Luke 11:37–41

Wednesday 17 October
Galatians 5:18–end
Psalm 1
Luke 11:42–6

Thursday 18 October
Isaiah 35:3–6
Psalm 147:1–7
Luke 10:1–9

Friday 19 October
Ephesians 1:11–14
Psalm 33:1–6, 12
Luke 12:1–7

Saturday 20 October
Ephesians 1:15–end
Psalm 8
Luke 12:8–12

Sunday 21 October
Job 38:1–7, 34–end
Psalm 104:1–10, 26, 35c
Hebrews 5:1–10
Mark 10:35–45

Monday 22 October
Ephesians 2:1–10
Psalm 100
Luke 12:13–21

Tuesday 23 October
Ephesians 2:12–end
Psalm 85:7–end
Luke 12:35–8

Wednesday 24 October
Ephesians 3:2–12
Psalm 98
Luke 12:39–48

Thursday 25 October
Ephesians 3:14–end
Psalm 33:1–6
Luke 12:49–53

Friday 26 October
Ephesians 4:1–6
Psalm 24:1–6
Luke 12:54–end

Saturday 27 October
Ephesians 4:7–16
Psalm 122
Luke 13:1–9

Sunday 28 October
Job 42:1–6, 10–end
Psalm 34:1–8, 14–end
Hebrews 7:23–end
Mark 10:46–end

Monday 29 October
Ephesians 4:32–5:8
Psalm 1
Luke 13:10–17

Tuesday 30 October
Ephesians 5:21–end
Psalm 128
Luke 13:18–21

Wednesday 31 October
Ephesians 6:1–9
Psalm 145:10–20
Luke 13:22–30

Thursday 1 November
Ephesians 6:10–20
Psalm 144:1–2, 9–11
Luke 13:31–end

Friday 2 November
Philippians 1:1–11
Psalm 111
Luke 14:1–6

Saturday 3 November
Philippians 1:18–26
Psalm 42:1–7
Luke 14:1, 7–11

Sunday 4 November
Isaiah 25:6–9
Psalm 24:1–6
Revelation 21:1–6a
John 11:32–44

Monday 5 November
Philippians 2:1–4
Psalm 131
Luke 14:12–14

Tuesday 6 November
Philippians 2:5–11
Psalm 22:22–7
Luke 14:15–24

Wednesday 7 November
Philippians 2:12–18
Psalm 27:1–5
Luke 14:25–33

Thursday 8 November
Philippians 3:3–8*a*
Psalm 105:1–7
Luke 15:1–10

Friday 9 November
Philippians 3:17—4:1
Psalm 122
Luke 16:1–8

Saturday 10 November
Philippians 4:10–19
Psalm 112
Luke 16:9–15

Sunday 11 November
Remembrance
Ruth 1:1–18
Psalm 146
Hebrews 9:11–14
Mark 12:28–34

Monday 12 November
Titus 1:1–9
Psalm 24:1–6
Luke 17:1–6

Tuesday 13 November
Titus 2:1–8, 11–14
Psalm 37:3–5, 30–2
Luke 17:7–10

Wednesday 14 November
Titus 3:1–7
Psalm 23
Luke 17:11–19

Thursday 15 November
Philemon 7–20
Psalm 146:4–end
Luke 17:20–5

Friday 16 November
2 John 4–9
Psalm 119:1–8
Luke 17:26–end

Saturday 17 November
3 John 5–8
Psalm 112
Luke 18:1–8

Sunday 18 November
Daniel 12:1–3
Psalm 16
Hebrews 10:11–25
Mark 13:1–8

Monday 19 November
Revelation 1:1–4; 2:1–5
Psalm 1
Luke 18:35–end

Tuesday 20 November
Revelation 3:1–6, 14–end
Psalm 15
Luke 19:1–10

Wednesday 21 November
Revelation 4
Psalm 150
Luke 19:11–28

Thursday 22 November
Revelation 5:1–10
Psalm 149:1–5
Luke 19:41–4

Friday 23 November
Revelation 10:8–end
Psalm 119:65–72
Luke 19:45–end

Saturday 24 November
Revelation 11:4–12
Psalm 144:1–9
Luke 20:27–40

Sunday 25 November
Christ the King
Daniel 7:9–10, 13–14
Psalm 93
Revelation 1:4*b*–8
John 18:33–7

Monday 26 November
Revelation 14:1–5
Psalm 24:1–6
Luke 21:1–4

Tuesday 27 November
Revelation 14:14–19
Psalm 96
Luke 21:5–11

Wednesday 28 November
Revelation 15:1–4
Psalm 98
Luke 21:12–19

Thursday 29 November
Revelation 18:1–2, 21–3; 19:1–3, 9
Psalm 100
Luke 21:20–8

Friday 30 November
Isaiah 52:7–10
Psalm 19:1–6
Romans 10:12–18
Matthew 4:18–22

Saturday 1 December
Revelation 22:1–7
Psalm 95:1–7
Luke 21:34–6

Acknowledgments

Pray Now 2012 was prepared by members of the Pray Now Writing Group: Peggy Roberts, Ishbel McFarlane, Carol Ford, Tina Kemp, Owain Jones, MaryAnn Rennie and Graham Fender-Allison.

Scriptural quotations for all occurrences of verses in Ecclesiastes 3:1–8 are taken from the *New Revised Standard Version*, © 1989 Division of Christian Education of the National Council of Churches of Christ in the United States of America, published by Oxford University Press.

Headline Scripture quotations are taken from THE HOLY BIBLE, NEW INTERNATIONAL VERSION®, NIV® Copyright © 1973, 1978, 1984, 2011 by Biblica, Inc.™ Used by permission. All rights reserved worldwide.

The Revised Common Lectionary is copyright © the Consultation on Common Texts, 1992 and is reproduced with permission. The Church of England's adapted form of *The Revised Common Lectionary*, published as the Principal Service Lectionary in *Common Worship: Services and Prayers for the Church of England*, the Second and Third Service Lectionaries and the *Common Worship* Calendar, also published in the same publication, and the Lectionaries for Certain Lesser Festivals, Common of the Saints and Special Occasions, published in the annual *Common Worship Lectionary*, are copyright © The Archbishops' Council of the Church of England, 1995, 1997. The *Common Worship* Weekday Lectionary is copyright © The Archbishops' Council, 2005. Material from these works is reproduced with permission.

We would like to extend our sincere thanks in particular to the Wild Goose Resource Group for their kind permission to reproduce parts of the following:

FOR ALL THE SAINTS (TLJ)
From THE LAST JOURNEY (Wild Goose Publications, 1996)
Words John L. Bell
Copyright © 1996 WGRG, Iona Community, Glasgow G2 3DH, Scotland

DANCE AND SING
From HEAVEN SHALL NOT WAIT (Wild Goose Publications, 1987)
Words John L. Bell and Graham Maule
Copyright © 1987 WGRG, Iona Community, Glasgow G2 3DH, Scotland

WE CANNOT MEASURE
From LOVE FROM BELOW (Wild Goose Publications, 1989)
Words John L. Bell and Graham Maule
Copyright © 1989 WGRG, Iona Community, Glasgow G2 3DH,
    Scotland

COME TAKE MY HAND
From ENEMY OF APATHY (Wild Goose Publications, 1988)
Words John L. Bell and Graham Maule
Copyright © 1988 WGRG, Iona Community, Glasgow G2 3DH,
    Scotland

SING HEY (Come with me, come wander)
From HEAVEN SHALL NOT WAIT (Wild Goose Publications, 1987)
Words John L. Bell and Graham Maule
Copyright © 1987 WGRG, Iona Community, Glasgow G2 3DH,
    Scotland

WGRG/Wild Goose Resource Group is a semi-autonomous project of the Iona Community, a charity registered in Scotland, No. SC003794.

The titles (books and CDs) containing the complete version of the above, among other resources for prayer and worship, can be obtained at www.wgrg.co.uk

Contact Us

For further information about *Pray Now* and other publications from the Church of Scotland's Faith Expressions Team, contact:

Faith Expressions Team
Mission and Discipleship Council
Church of Scotland
121 George Street
Edinburgh EH2 4YN

Tel: 0131 225 5722
Fax: 0131 220 3113

e-mail: mandd@cofscotland.org.uk